ENDORSEME

Honest, personal, practical, and provocative—*Contagious Disciple-Making* closely examines classic ministry models against God's kingdom values, and also against God's unchanging goals of transformed and reproducing disciples. David Watson has had a major role in catalyzing more than sixty disciple making movements across the globe, which is why this book will meet a great need in the 21st century church. If you really want to radically change your world, then David and Paul's book may irrevocably change your life!

—**Jerry Trousdale**, Author of *Miraculous Movements: How Hundreds of Thousands of Muslims are Falling in Love with Jesus*

The best work I've seen on creating viral movements for the gospel. *Contagious Disciple-Making* is inspirational, Biblical, and highly practical. This could be the seismic shift the Western Church needs to move in power through the 21st Century.

—**Erik Fish**, Author of *Disciple* and founder of DiscipleX

This long-awaited book by David and Paul Watson fulfills the promise to radically impact all who read it. A powerful blend of the prophetic and the practical, *Contagious Disciple-Making*, is rooted in reality. I have personally encountered the disciples and new communities of faith that have accompanied the Watson's ministry and training all over the world. May God use the message of this book to transform your ministry, as it has my own.

—**David Garrison**, Missionary and Author

David Watson has simply, modestly and ruthlessly prodded me to de-culturize my reading of the Bible and deconstruct the theology of disciple-making that came with my errant ways. Seeing the activities of Jesus recorded in the Bible without my western eyes has catalyzed a new way of disciple-making. I have a new hope and confidence that the Great Commission can be accomplished. What a gift to the Bride of Christ to have this book as a guide to this new way of disciple-making. *Contagious Disciple-Making* should be required reading for every follower of Christ who is serious about the Great Commission.

—**Roy Moran**, Author of *Spent Matches*, Thomas Nelson 2015

In late 2008, David and Paul Watson travelled to Honduras to train our organization's missionaries and indigenous leaders. The principles and tactics that they taught and modeled were transformational in the lives of that small disciple making team. Those Honduran leaders began to adapt the disciple making practices they were using with about 25 small groups. David and Paul continued to serve as mentors to us as our team began to live and practice these Biblical principles. Today there are about 700 groups and churches that have multiplied from this beginning, and more importantly, thousands of new obedient disciples of Jesus Christ in Honduras and some of the surrounding countries.

Now in this book, *Contagious Disciple-Making*, that same training is available to everyone. This is a book that can be read and re-read. It is the same practical teaching that our team received. I believe that as people put these principles into practice, new disciples will be made, new groups and churches will be multiplied, and new movements of Christ followers will emerge.

—**David Parish**, President, World Missions and Evangelism, Inc.

Hopefully this new/ancient contagion will go viral! It is the only viable disciple making strategy that has the potential of fulfilling Christ's command. No surprise, since it came from Jesus and his first disciples. David and Paul focus on its biblical origin; the dominant role of the Holy Spirit and the necessity of personal obedience. This writing fully documents how mentoring new disciples results in explosive multiplication. From trial and error they define strategy and describe how tactics can be developed. A must read for any serious disciple-maker, whether in Jerusalem or the ends of the earth.

—**R. Keith Parks**, Retired President, Foreign Mission Board (International Mission Board), Southern Baptist Convention. Retired Global Missions Coordinator, Cooperative Baptist Fellowship

Most Christians want to make disciples, but do not know how. *Contagious Disciple-Making* shows them how every believer can be a disciple-maker of disciple-makers. The Watsons do a masterful job of showing how easy disciple-making is (everyone can do it) and how hard disciple-making is (God calls us to deep changes in our mind and heart and lifestyle).

Contagious Disciple-Making is a must-read for followers of Jesus who want to be transformed by God to transform the world. This book is a good mix of Biblical basis, challenges to self-evaluate, practical application and faith-building stories of how God is using "ordinary people" to do extraordinary things.

Find a group of friends and use *Contagious Disciple-Making* as a guidebook to see God do "far more than you can ask or imagine" to reach those living hopeless lives without Jesus.

—**Stan Parks**, Disciple and Disciple Making Movements Servant, VP Global Strategies, Act Beyond (Beyond.org)

I have had the unique privilege of being David Watson's pastor for the last five years. Little did I know when I first met David how the stories and ideas presented in this book (many of which were shared with me over lunchtime conversations) would dramatically impact my views on disciple-making. I enthusiastically recommend this anointed book by anointed men who are seeing God do miraculous works across the globe.

—**Dr. Larry Parsley**, Senior Pastor, Valley Ranch Baptist Church, Coppell, TX

Contagious Disciple-Making is an incredible book that will help a believer to discover Christ and have a lasting relationship of following Christ as His disciple. My journey with both David and Paul Watson in Disciple Making Movements and training, together have impacted my own world and today, by God's grace, we have a record of thousands of disciples who are making disciples transforming their villages and cities. This is a book to be read by all. It will change your world.

—**Dr. Aila Tasse**, President of Lifeway Mission International (Nairobi, Kenya)

I have been an aspiring disciple maker for 48 years. And I have read just about every book there is on the subject of discipleship. But David and Paul Watson have brought together in this one book more insights and more practical wisdom than most books on this topic put together. This is a must read for followers of Jesus who want to see the world turned upside-down for Christ.

—**Floyd McClung**, www.floydandsally.com, Cape Town, South Africa

The Watsons have provided us with an excellent and comprehensive picture of disciplemaking. This book is a superb guide for every ministry leader. The principles of making disciples are addressed from depth of experience, making it very workable. They help us identify and clear out our cultural issues and practices that obstruct the furtherance of the Gospel, and then they show us how to help grow new believers, grow existing churches and plant new churches. I strongly recommend this highly effective and powerful tool to help advance the Kingdom of God!

—**Dr. Doug Shaw**, President and CEO of International Students, Inc.

CONTAGIOUS DISCIPLE-MAKING

DAVID L. WATSON
AND PAUL D. WATSON

THOMAS NELSON
Since 1798

NASHVILLE   MEXICO CITY   RIO DE JANEIRO

Published in Nashville, Tennessee, by Thomas Nelson. Thomas Nelson is a trademark of HarperCollins Christian Publishing.

Page design and layout: Crosslin Creative

Thomas Nelson titles may be purchased in bulk for educational, business, fund-raising, or sales promotional use. For information, please e-mail SpecialMarkets@ThomasNelson.com.

Unless otherwise indicated, Scripture quotations are taken from the Holy Bible, New International Version®, NIV®. Copyright © 1973, 1978, 1984, 2011 by Biblica, Inc.® Used by permission of Zondervan. All rights reserved worldwide. www.zondervan.com

Scripture quotations marked ESV are from THE ENGLISH STANDARD VERSION. © 2001 by Crossway Bibles, a division of Good News Publishers.

Scripture quotations marked NASB are from the NEW AMERICAN STANDARD BIBLE®, © The Lockman Foundation 1960, 1962, 1963, 1968, 1971, 1972, 1973, 1975, 1977, 1995. Used by permission.

ISBN: 9780529112200

Printed in the United States of America

14 15 16 17 18 19 RRD 6 5 4 3 2 1

DEDICATIONS

From David:

This book is dedicated to my wife, Jan, who has spent half of our 41+ years of marriage wondering where in the world I was and if I would make it back home or not. She has been a sounding board for the ideas in this book, and is my most faithful and loving critic. Without her sacrifice, love and support this book would have never happened because the work it is based on would have never happened.

This book is also dedicated to my mentees who have taught me far more than I ever taught them. Included in this incredible group of men are my sons, Paul and Jonathan. You make me proud!

From Paul:

To my mom and dad, without you I wouldn't be the man I am today.

To my wife, Christi, and my children, Yahel, John Paul, and Keturah, I look forward to seeing you each and every day. You fill me with joy.

To the hundreds of men and women who have died in the service of our King, you inspire me and challenge me to live a life completely dedicated to bringing honor and glory to Christ.

CONTENTS

INTRODUCTION

God, I can't plant churches anymore. I didn't sign on to love people, train people, send people, and get them killed.

Six men I (David) had worked with had been martyred over the last eighteen months.

I can't live in the area You called me to reach.

The Indian government expelled our family from the country. More than twenty-five hundred miles and an ocean separated our house in Singapore from the Bhojpuri people in North India.

The task is too big.

There were 80 million Bhojpuri living in an area known as the "graveyard of missions and missionaries."

There isn't enough help.

There were only twenty-seven evangelical churches in the area. They struggled to survive. Fewer than a thousand believers lived among the Bhojpuri at that time.

Take away my call. I will go back to the States. I'm good at business. I will give lots of money to missions. Let someone else plant churches. Let me go. Release me from my call.

Every day for two months we had the same conversation. Every day I went to my office, sat in the dark, and begged God to take away my call. And every day He refused.

Fine. You have to teach me how to plant churches. I cannot believe that You would call someone to a task without telling him how to do it. Show me in Your Word how You want me to reach these people. If You show me, I will do it.

This was my covenant with God. This is what started my part in the work among the Bhojpuri.

NEW IDEAS

God upheld His part of our covenant. Over the next year, He led me through Scripture and brought my attention to things I had read but never understood—at least in this context. Patterns emerged and new thoughts about church, making disciples, and church planting came to life.

I prayed for five Indian men to help develop these ideas in North India. I met the first at a secret forum gathered in India to discuss evangelizing Hindus. They invited me to present some of my ideas. As I talked, they started leaving. One by one, two by two, sometimes five at a time, people got up and left the room. They thought I was crazy! By the end of the day, only one remained.

"I believe what you're saying," he told me. "I can see it too."

We talked long into the night and became friends. He became the first to help me develop these ideas. Over the next year, three other men emerged to work with me.

"Lord," I prayed, "where is the fifth man? Where is the one we need to complete our team?"

Now, this was in the days when people still wrote letters. I got stacks of them every day. In Singapore the mail carriers rode motor scooters that had a very distinct sound. I heard the mailman putter up to my gate and drop the mail in the box. That day I got a letter from India, from someone I didn't know.

"Brother David," it began, "You don't know me, but I feel God telling me that I should become your disciple. Tell me what to do, and I will do it." Here was the fifth member of my team. But God didn't give me the man I prayed for. You see, a woman wrote the letter I got that day.

Over the next few years, we struggled as we implemented the things God taught us. Our first church planted with this new methodology didn't happen until two years after the secret forum. In fact, the mission organization I worked for threatened to fire me each year during my annual review.

"You're not doing your job," they said.

"Give me time," I responded. "We're trying something new. Trust me." And for some reason, they did.

All of a sudden, we saw eight churches planted in one year. The next year, there were 48 new churches planted. The year after that, 148, then 327, and then 500. In the fifth year, we saw more than 1,000 new churches planted!

After the fifth year, my mission organization called me: "You must be mistaken," they insisted. "No one can plant 1,000 churches in one year. We didn't believe 500, but we certainly don't believe 1,000!"

"Come and see," I told them. And they did. A formal survey of the work among the Bhojpuri showed that our team actually underreported the number of churches planted in the area! By 2008, another survey of the work revealed 80,000 churches planted and 2 million people baptized. Things were exploding!

In 1999 I left the organization that sent me to India and continued the work in India under the ministry name I had used to establish the work. By 2004 the work in India was entirely indigenously led and did not need me anymore. Cityteam, a well-established organization with fifty-plus-year history of helping the homeless and addicted find and follow Jesus, decided they wanted to become an organization that catalyzed Disciple-Making Movements as they met the needs of people in extreme circumstances. We decided to work together on a pilot project in Africa.

The pilot project grew from Sierra Leone to include thirty-three African nations. At the time of writing this introduction, nine years into the project, our teams have started 26,911 churches and baptized 933,717 people. You can read more about Cityteam and our work in Africa in the book *Miraculous Movements: How Hundreds of Thousands of Muslims Are Falling in Love with Jesus,* by our colleague Jerry Trousdale.

In spite of living and traveling all over the globe, we've never forgotten the lost people living and dying in the United States of America. Cityteam continues its work among the homeless and addicted while seeking to catalyze Disciple-Making Movements in America. At the time of writing this chapter, 1,296 Discovery Groups have been started in fourteen states. The work there has spread through relational lines from Latino families in the United States to families in South and Central America. There are 626 Discovery Groups and 25 churches in twelve countries in Central and South America.

———————— 🌐 ————————

I (Paul) never intended to plant churches like my father does. There was a time when I thought God had called me into ministry, but a brief and unsuccessful attempt as a youth minister made me question that call. I dabbled in business, but basically wandered from thing to thing, not sure what I wanted to do with my life. Eventually, Dad roped me into a couple of writing and curriculum development projects with Cityteam. I could write, I knew the subject matter, and I was relatively cheap labor.

While working for Cityteam, I experimented with the ideas and concepts Dad and I talk about in this book. I am an experimenter by nature, and I wanted to know if the concepts I was writing about would work in a real world of someone who had a job, a marriage, children, hobbies, and a church. They did. And eventually God clearly called me to make disciples and develop disciple-makers and Disciple-making Teams worldwide.

Cityteam hired me, and the real adventure began.

I've traveled more than 185,000 miles—around the world and throughout the United States—training Disciple-makers and their teams. When I couldn't physically visit a place, I used Skype and a cell phone to train Disciple-makers. As a result, these Disciple-makers found Persons of Peace and started Discovery Groups all over the world.

Toward the end of 2011, Cityteam asked me to become the city director of Cityteam's Recovery Center in Portland, Oregon. Through our Recovery Center, we feed seventy-two thousand meals a year (six thousand per month). We help, on average, 84 people per night, 365 days per year, get showers, find clothing, and a have a place to sleep. I am responsible for leading the team in Portland as we meet the physical needs of the homeless, addicted, and alcoholic while seeking to catalyze Disciple-Making Movements in the Pacific Northwest.

David and I are very different. He is a thinker. I am a feeler. He is an extreme introvert (although few realize it), and I am an extreme extrovert. He played football in high school, and I sang competitively. Yet, even with all of these differences, there is one burning question that unites us: How do we help the millions of lost people who will never step foot inside the doors of existing churches fall in love with Jesus? When David and I sit in our churches here in the United States, we can't keep from looking around and mourning over all the lost people who aren't there and, if we continue to try to get them to fit into our Christian culture, will never come. If you find yourself asking the same question and struggling with the same feelings, this book is for you.

Everything you read in this book comes from our personal experience and the experiences of those we train. If God has called you to catalyze Disciple-Making Movements, we hope this book helps you fulfill that call. If God has called you to something else, we hope you find ideas in this book that will help you as you obey your own unique call.

Let the adventure begin!

PART
1

THE MIND-SET OF A
DISCIPLE-MAKER

DISCIPLE-MAKERS EMBRACE LESSONS TAUGHT BY FAILURE

I (David) participated in the meeting where the term *Church—Planting Movement* was coined. We—a group of mission practitioners and strategists—wanted to describe what we had observed in several countries as we took seriously our understanding of the Great Commission's charge to go and make disciples of all peoples, baptize them into local churches, and teach them to obey all the commands of Christ.

None of us, in our wildest dreams, ever thought we would witness what happened. Initially, our goals were to establish "beachhead" churches in resistant or inaccessible locations and people groups. We planned on establishing a single church where there was none. We had no plans for starting hundreds or thousands of churches. We didn't even dream it was possible to see that many churches started in the places where we worked. These places we were targeting had already demonstrated their resistance to the Gospel, to church planting, and to any other outside influence. We just did everything we could think of in hopes that something would work and at least one church would start. We defined success as one church started in a people group where there was none.

As one of the first in my denomination to take on this challenge, I had no clue how to make it happen. My wife and I were considered successful church planters because we took risks and tried new things. And, perhaps most important, because we were not afraid of failure. When we failed, we just tried something else.

Our organization trained us in good research skills. We discussed access and evangelism techniques. We developed prayer networks, security protocols, and communication and administration systems. As a result of research, I knew reaching the new people group could not depend on me, because I did not have access. This people group would not respond to outsiders because their history was full of wars resisting outside influence. What was I to do?

God taught me, through many failures, that I had to focus on making disciples of Christ, not followers of my church or denomination. He also taught me that I needed to teach these disciples to obey the commands of Jesus, not my church/denominational doctrines or traditions. This is what led to the breakthrough that resulted in more than eighty thousand churches among a people considered unreachable.

Initially, the term *Church-Planting Movement* meant "spontaneous churches starting without the missionary's direct involvement." Over time, my teammates and I decided to quantify and qualify the term to be a bit more specific for the church planters we trained, coached, and mentored. We defined a Church-Planting Movement as an indigenously led Gospel-planting and obedience-based discipleship process that resulted in a minimum of one hundred new locally initiated and led churches, four generations deep, within three years. Paul and I will go into greater detail about all the elements of this definition later. At the time of this writing, there are sixty-eight movements among people groups around the world.

As more and more leaders became practitioners of the methodologies that lead to a CPM, they had a couple of observations. First, they realized people have different definitions of church. In some cases, people became angry because what we reported as a church did not match their definition of one. The word *church* did not communicate what we thought it would. People challenged our practitioners, saying, "Jesus said He would build the church. Why do you have people focused on doing something Jesus said He would do?" These were good observations, and we needed to address them.

After a lot of conversations, we decided to use the term *Disciple-Making Movement*, or *DMM*, to describe our role in God's redemptive work. There is no doubt that we have a role. Matthew 28:16–20, the Great Commission, tells us to make disciples. The implication is that these disciples would also make disciples, and so on.

As believers obey Christ, they are to train men and women to be Contagious Disciple-Makers who pray, engage lost communities, find Persons of Peace (the ones God has prepared to receive the Gospel in a community for the first time), help them discover Jesus through Discovery Groups (an inductive group Bible study process designed to take people from not knowing Christ to falling in love with Him), baptize new believers, help them become communities of faith called church, and mentor emerging leaders. All of these very intentional activities catalyze Disciple-Making Movements. Jesus works through His people as they obey His Word, a Disciple-Making Movement becomes a Church-Planting Movement, and Jesus gets the glory for everything.

Many people use the term *Church-Planting Movement* or *Disciple-Making Movement* to describe or justify what they do. But on closer examination, Paul and I find that many groups who use one of these terms simply apply it to what they have always done. In our experience, a CPM is the result of obedience-based discipleship that sees disciples reproducing disciples, leaders reproducing leaders, and churches reproducing churches—in other words, a Disciple-Making Movement. If these things are not happening, it is not a CPM.

True DMM methodology is about being disciplined in educating, training, and mentoring people to obey all the commands of Jesus, regardless of consequences. The results are not quick. They only appear to be so because of exponential growth. When we truly engage in the process that leads to an observable DMM, we typically spend two to four years discipling and developing leaders. But because of the replication process due to leaders being taught to obey God's Word by making disciples and teaching them to obey, in this same two to four years as many as five more leaders emerge. These leaders also develop more leaders. Each leader invests two to four years in other leaders, who invest two to four years in other leaders, and so on. The apparent result is explosive growth that does not seem to take much time and energy. But appearances are misleading.

DMMs are extremely time and energy intensive. Leaders invest a major portion of their time equipping other leaders. Churches invest in starting more groups that become churches as they obey Christ's teachings and fulfill the nature and functions of church, which means they teach others to do the same.

There were no visible or measurable results the first four years of my ministry among a very resistant unreached people group. My mission organization was ready to discipline me for failure to do my job. But during those years I equipped five leaders. These five equipped twenty-five more, who in turn equipped hundreds of other leaders.

A few churches became more churches as leaders were equipped and trained to obey all the commands of Christ. More churches became hundreds of churches as the leadership equipping process continued. Every leader has years invested in him or her by other leaders. Nothing is quick. It only appears to be because more and more leaders are being produced in obedience to Christ's command to "go and make disciples of all nations, baptizing them in the name of the Father and of the Son and of the Holy Spirit, and teaching them to obey everything I have commanded you" (Matt. 28:19–20).

So, in a DMM, rapid multiplication really isn't rapid. We go slowly, but appear to go fast. We invest extensively in one person to reach and train many. We want to add at least two new leaders to our mentoring process each year, and equip the new leaders to do the same every year. As leaders multiply, churches grow and multiply.

If you really want to start a Disciple-Making Movement anywhere in the world and witness God's work as He starts a Church-Planting Movement, invest in teaching, training, and mentoring leaders to obey all the commands of Christ. If you want to evaluate a so-called DMM, examine the discipleship and leadership-equipping process. Real and lasting DMMs invest heavily in leadership and training. A DMM is causative; a CPM is the result.

DISCIPLE-MAKERS DECULTURALIZE, NOT CONTEXTUALIZE, THE GOSPEL

When I was five, my Sunday school teacher handed me a piece of paper and some crayons and asked me to draw a picture of Jesus. My church was not one to have images of Jesus hanging or standing around, though I am sure I must have seen some renditions of Jesus in books, in Bibles, or hanging on the walls around my community. When I finished my assignment to the best of my young and untrained abilities, my Jesus looked exactly like me in the ways that count. He had white skin, blond hair, and blue eyes. I loved Jesus, and was proud of how I had drawn Him.

As a college student I was involved in the missions program of my student union. I was assigned to work among a group of young African American students in my community. It was my first cross-cultural experience.

One day I exhausted all my materials before the time was up, so I grabbed some paper, colored pencils, and crayons and passed them out. I instructed the children to draw a picture of Jesus. I was surprised when their pictures depicted a Jesus with dark skin and African features.

Since those early days in my ministry, I have been fascinated with how various cultures depict Jesus. I have worked with Hispanics, American Indians, East Asians, South Asians,

Southeast Asians, Middle Easterners, and Africans. Children from each culture will render Jesus as looking like themselves unless taught to do differently. This is natural, and I think it is a part of God's plan for reaching the nations. Jesus is no longer flesh and blood, as we know. He is different from us. Now we meet Him as the Holy Spirit represents Him to us. He has no color, no ethnic heritage, and no cultural distinctions except the holiness and righteousness of God.

One of the challenges of being a cross-cultural witness is presenting Jesus in the same way the Holy Spirit would. Jesus' cultural heritage is the family of God. As the Creator, He made all of us, regardless of our cultural identity, in His own image. As His adopted children we have a responsibility to become like Him. We should not introduce Jesus as looking or being like us. He is not. To represent Him as something He is not is a lie, first to ourselves, and then to those we wish to introduce to Him.

Since 1977, I have given my life to the ministry of cross-cultural witness on behalf of Jesus. In the early days I was trained to contextualize my witness to my host culture. As I understood contextualization, this was basically to make Jesus acceptable to them by dressing Him up to look like them. Add a little makeup, change the clothes, use a different language, and voilà: a Jesus they certainly couldn't refuse.

But with time, the makeup I applied began to run. The clothes wore out. And the language was always something short of perfect. The Jesus as I understood Him would ultimately show up, confusing and sometimes offending my hosts.

Regardless of how hard I tried, I could never make Jesus look just right to another culture. Even though I have had some success in presenting my made-up Jesus to my hosts, it was extremely difficult and tiring to keep the makeup fresh, the clothes new, and the language just right. No matter how diligently I studied and researched culture and built relationships, I could not know my host culture well enough to present Jesus in a perfectly contextualized manner. My clothes, food choices, and language, as well as adopted cultural forms of family relations, community involvement, and worship, were always slightly off at best, disastrous at worst.

I began to question contextualization. Perhaps I just wasn't cut out to be a cross-cultural witness for Jesus. I began to pray that God would show me how to represent Him to others. And slowly, as all good teachers do, God began to teach me through others' experiences, my own experiences, and object lessons that I will never forget.

Since 1985 I have been working in the unreached and least-reached parts of our world. I have had to work in secret, and I have had to keep my identity well hidden. Anything less could have resulted in the loss of access to the people to whom God sent me, as well as the deaths of those who accepted Christ as a result of my witness. A dressed-up Jesus was not an option. I was nonresidential much of the time and didn't have the time or the inclination to keep the makeup straight, the clothes new, and the language perfect. I had to learn another way.

My first learning experience came when I had the unique opportunity to witness to a member of my host community. He was an old shopkeeper who was well liked and had no problems with me as a foreigner. We conversed almost daily. I liked him, and I think he liked me. I did not hide the fact that I was a Christian. Everyone assumed I was anyway, since I was white. He did not hide the fact that he was a Hindu.

One day our conversation strayed to religion. As a trained witness I was thrilled with the opportunity. But as it turned out, the opportunity was one for me to learn, not to lead another person into the Kingdom of God.

The old man told me that he just did not understand Christianity. There was no way he could give up his religion, which was so much a part of his daily life, to accept a new religion that from his perspective was so much NOT a part of the daily lives of the Christians he knew. He began every day with meditations, offerings, and prayers to his god. As the day went on, he would stop for more prayer and meditation. Each business transaction was blessed in prayer, and each dollar made thankfully offered to his god.

Everyone knew his devotion, and that devotion was as obvious at home and in private as it was in public. The questions he presented to me shoved me into some long and deep thought and prayer.

"Why would I want to give up the god I can see for one I cannot see?"

"Why would I want to worship only one day a week when now I worship several times every day?"

"Why would I want to do business without the presence of my god to oversee it and bless it?"

"Why would I want to try to convince others of my holiness with words, when they can see my devotion to my god?"

"Why would I want to let only words teach my children, rather than my life?"

This old man had a limited and distorted view of a committed Christian's life, but the form of secret or private worship that was the norm for most Christians he knew or observed was certainly contributing to his misunderstanding. I realized this had to change. I asked God to give me a local cultural informant who could take Jesus as I know Him and present the essence of who He is in a meaningful way to this man's culture.

As I prayed for this person, I realized that I had to find a way to minimize my cultural representation of Jesus. This is quite different from dressing Jesus up in a way that would be acceptable to another culture. How can I ever know another culture well enough to dress Jesus up to meet their expectations, wants, or needs? I cannot. But I do know my own culture, and if I am honest with Scripture and critical in my thinking and planning, I can present Jesus in a near-acultural way that can be assimilated and transformed into a cultural model by the ones God has chosen and prepared. I have learned that God has prepared men and women in every culture who can meet those who love Jesus from another culture, learn to love Jesus from them, strip away the cultural baggage attached (which we can minimize), and present Jesus to their own culture in a loving and caring way that results in lives changed and the Kingdom enlarged.

The most obvious areas where I needed to strip away my own culture and cultural expectations were in my worship styles, both private and public. As I taught my new friends worship, I taught the elements of worship, not a style or form. This was not easy. What was natural for me was foreign for them. I learned to ask questions as I taught.

When I introduced prayer, I asked them how they would pray. They began to pray in a way that was familiar to them and directed toward the God we all knew and loved. When I introduced singing, I asked them what songs they would sing. They had none, so I did not give them one of mine. Instead, the Holy Spirit inspired them to write their own. It sounded like their music, and it gave glory and honor to God.

When I introduced teaching, I asked them how they would teach God's Word. Their style was different from mine, but normal for their culture. When I introduced preaching, I asked them how they would exhort others to follow Christ's teachings. The resulting form of preaching was different from what I was used to, but it met their needs and was acceptable to their culture. When I introduced church leadership, I asked them how they would lead a group in their community. The results were different from the congregational approach I would have taken, but it fit them and their way of doing things.

For my new friends, worship and church were a daily and daylong lifestyle that was apparent to their community. It was despised by some and spoken against by others, but was much more acceptable to the community than anything I could have presented to them or lived out before them. It had impact.

Regardless of how careful one is to deculturalize one's message, there are teachings in the Bible that are simply against cultural norms. For instance, in a culture where the norm is multiple wives, the teaching of one wife for life is difficult to accept. In these situations one must teach God's Word, but, more important, teach that all of us are to obey God's Word. The Great Commission (Matt. 28:19–20) includes the admonition that we are to teach others to obey everything Christ has commanded. I have learned that teaching doctrine and teaching obedience are two very different things.

I went overseas with all kinds of doctrinal material to present to the new believers. I discovered that doctrine was another area where cultural baggage can be found. Doctrine is basically a church's or denomination's teachings on what they believe the Bible says and how it is to be lived out (in their own culture). Doctrine often includes forms and traditions that are outside the biblical context, though acceptable within the biblical and cultural context under which the doctrine was developed. Church polity, church staff, ordinations, the practices of baptism and the Lord's Supper, the teachings regarding clergy and laity, and more can carry significant cultural baggage that may be extrabiblical without being disobedient to the Scripture in a given culture. The cross-cultural witness must be able to identify the cultural areas and eliminate them from his or her teachings. The best way to do this is to use only Scripture for curricula, and allow local people to answer questions about Scripture, not listen to our answers. We have to learn to teach by asking a minimal number of questions, not by giving the answers to every question or having an expressed opinion about everything.

Our focus in discipleship has become obedience to the Gospel, not adherence to a doctrine. With a doctrine-centered discipleship program, one must teach everything to ensure a person has the knowledge to be obedient. With an obedience-centered discipleship program, the emphasis is on how we can be obedient to Christ in every area of our lives and in every circumstance. When a new disciple asks a question, my answer is always the same: What must you do to be obedient to Christ? I may have to help that person find the appropriate passages in the Bible to answer the question, but the question always remains the same. In this form of teaching, faith is defined as being obedient to the commands of Christ in every situation or circumstance, regardless of the consequences.

During one baptism the village leader was visibly agitated. He and his family were to be baptized, but as the time approached, he became more agitated and even angry and was overheard mumbling, "This is wrong" and "This is evil." A wise worker allowed him to voice his feelings and then asked him to explain what it was about the baptism that was wrong or evil. The village leader explained that it was wrong for a man from outside the family to touch the women in his family. The doctrinal teaching was that an ordained minister should administer baptism. The worker was quick to ask himself the question, *how can I be obedient to the teaching of Christ in this?* He quickly asked the leader if it would be appropriate for him to baptize the leader, and then the leader could baptize the rest of the new believers. He made a change, and the baptism continued.

We learned that the form of baptism we had been practicing was a hindrance to the spread of the Gospel. Many women were refusing to be baptized because a man other than a family member would be touching them. Baptism by ordained ministers was not a requirement of the Bible, but was simply a tradition of the church. With a simple change in form, baptisms increased from a few each month to tens if not hundreds each week. What's more, the leadership transferred to the village was significant. Many who may have stayed on the fringe of the work became key leaders as they accepted the spiritual responsibility of baptizing their families, and went on to become the true spiritual leaders in their homes and villages.

As you may have discerned, baptism in the area we were serving is primarily done with the entire family. The Gospel is presented to families through a discovery process. This avoids extraction evangelism, and conversions usually result in a church being established. A child or a woman may be the door into the family, but the head of the household usually leads the whole family into the decision to follow Christ. This is different from some cultures, but if we had maintained the traditional individual conversion approach, the church's growth would have been hampered.

There are more examples of how form and practice from one culture may have a negative or neutral impact on another culture. You probably have many examples from your own ministry. Part of the job of the cross-cultural witness is to eliminate the cultural aspects of his or her own understanding of doctrine and practice and to help those in the host culture discover biblically acceptable ways of expressing their own love, devotion, and worship of the Lord Jesus Christ.

So the question remains: What color is Jesus? For the cross-cultural witness the color is always neutral. When Christ is in the culture, He will look just like the members of that culture. He will represent God and His righteousness to the culture. He will become the measuring stick by which everyone in the culture is measured. His Word will be obeyed, and their love will be made complete.

The role of the cross-cultural worker is to *deculturalize* the Gospel—presenting the Gospel without commentary, but with the question, "How will we obey what God has said?" If it's not in the Bible, don't introduce it to the culture. The role of the cultural worker is also to *contextualize* the Gospel—presenting the Gospel and asking, "What must we change in our lives and culture in order to be obedient to all the commands of Christ?"

Working in your birth culture doesn't excuse you from relating to friends and family as a cross-cultural worker. Once you chose to follow Christ, your culture started to change. Your values changed. How you handle conflict changed. Your language may have changed. Your hobbies may have changed. Within two years of deciding to follow Christ, you can no longer relate to your birth culture as a cultural insider. You changed. Others remained.

If you have significant misunderstandings and disagreements as you try to include your friends and family in culturally Christian activities or conversations about your faith, then you are probably trying to relate to them as a cultural insider when you are not. You need to work on deculturalizing the Gospel so your friends and family can hear it without cultural baggage and have the opportunity to contextualize it.

DISCIPLE-MAKERS PLANT THE GOSPEL RATHER THAN REPRODUCE THEIR RELIGION

I never set out to start a house church movement. Even today, when I work with new people in new locations, the objective is not to start a house church movement but to meet and address lostness in every segment of society through the Gospel of Jesus Christ. I truly have no preconceived ideas of what form the local church takes as lostness is addressed, the Gospel is presented, families and affinity groups come to Christ, communities are transformed, and new churches are started. (More on this later.)

The church belongs to Christ, and He determines how the church grows and what it looks like. The body of believers certainly does its part, but Christ is the Head of the church. Different segments of society and different cultures put church together differently as they obey the Word and follow the guidance of the Holy Spirit in their own context. A disciple-maker's job is to present the Gospel as honestly and as aculturally as possible. As families, affinity groups, and individuals come to Christ, we teach and guide them by example and word to discover what the Bible has to say and to obey it. We do not think there is only one way to obey the mandates of the Word in connection to the church. (By this we mean not everyone must worship the same way, pray the same way, serve the same way, fast the same way, sing the same way, or do anything else the same way in order to be obedient to Christ.) As we obey the Word in our own context, there will be differences, but obedience continues. In some circumstances this may mean house church. In other situations it may lead to some other structure of church that is appropriate for that context.

Identifying our personal cultures—including our religious and nationalistic traditions—and keeping them from permeating new work is the single biggest hurdle we face. Our Christian culture can have an extremely negative impact on disciple-making. In our experience, fewer and fewer people want anything to do with Christian culture. In fact, Christian culture—not to be confused with God or what He teaches through the Bible—is often a barrier to people falling in love with Jesus. Additionally, fewer people want anything to do with anything that looks or feels religious. So we avoid "churchy" words, phrases, titles, and so forth. Most people in North America have been exposed to Christianity (although this is changing rapidly in our major cities), so it is not unusual for them to adopt the Christian cultural words when they describe what is happening to them or discuss religious experiences and ideas. But we let them make these determinations.

We do our best NOT to transfer our own Christian culture, denominational terms, or doctrine into the new work. By this we mean programs and processes that require:

- a focus on starting churches that adhere to and look like a particular church, denomination, or doctrinal position;

- a formalized and institutionalized educational process for all leadership;

- formal ordination of leadership that qualifies them to lead;

- high to strict control of the teaching/preaching ministries of the church and the ordinances of baptism and the Lord's Supper by ordained leaders;

- a high focus, in some cases, on having a building that is called "church"; and

- a high control of all aspects of church.

Please understand that we don't consider any of these wrong. Any organization or church has the right to determine how they will do church and what qualifies individuals and groups to be considered a part of the denomination, organization, or church. But many of these requirements are extra-biblical and slow church planting in such a way that natural replication cannot happen. And simply renaming what one has been doing for years as a Church Planting Movement, a Disciple-Making Movement, or Contagious Disciple Making does not make it so.

Of course, this got me into trouble with my denomination. They wanted all new work to look and act like the rest of the denomination, even though this was a barrier in the past and continues to be a barrier as new people engage the Gospel. Statistics show that traditional church is losing ground to population growth.[1] Although some still find their spiritual needs met in spaces defined by Christian culture—whether institutional or house church—an ever-increasing number of people reject that culture and are looking for something different.

Deculturalizing is difficult. We continually battle our Christian culture when we make disciples. We often work in the traditional Christian culture world one day, and in an anti-Christian world the next day. I spent from 1973 to 1997 working in a denominational setting. Ignoring, reversing, or changing twenty-five years of cultural immersion is difficult, but I choose to continue working on it. The less religious I am and more spiritual I am, the more effective I become as a disciple-maker.

We must never equate religion and spirituality. Religion is about how we do church. Spirituality is about how we live out our relationship with God and people in such a way that we, our families, and our communities are transformed. Lost people are mostly repulsed by religion but inexplicably drawn to spiritual men and women. When disciple-making, we strive to be less religious. In all settings, we want to continue to grow spiritually. By this we mean a deepening of our relationships to God through Jesus Christ and the power of the Holy Spirit that changes us and impacts our families and communities positively for Christ.

When we love people, they know it. What we do speaks much louder than our words, for it opens the ears of those who want to hear the words we have to speak. Love the people, and they will come to Christ as you minister to them and lead them to discover God for themselves.

DISCIPLE-MAKERS REALIZE HOW HARD COMPLETING THE GREAT COMMISSION WILL BE FOR STRATEGIES AND ORGANIZATIONS BUILT AROUND BRANDED CHRISTIANITY[1]

First of all, I (David) am not anti-denominational, antichurch, or anti–Christian organization. I spent more than fifteen years as a denominational employee and ten years in various denominational church staff roles, and have been a member of the same denomination for more than fifty years. Both Paul and I work for a Christian organization.

What we realize, however, is that organizations that promote a particular brand of Christianity will have difficulty completing the Great Commission. Historically, promoting branded Christianity has been the focus of denominations and their affiliated educational institutions. In some parts of the world, denominations are growing. In others, networks are rising up and taking their place. What distinguishes a branded Christian institution is the insistence that all related churches and any churches they start adhere to a particular and peculiar perspective and associated practices related to the Bible, as well as their particular group history. All branded Christianity–focused groups are Bible-based and history-based. They may require a strict or loose adherence to their doctrine and/or practices. Their doctrine, however, is at best a subset of what Scripture has to say, and at worst contains extrabiblical teachings and practices based on their church history. All worship styles, leadership styles, and governance styles are mostly extrabiblical, even though all denominations will claim a biblical background or basis for their practices.

Groups that promote a particular brand of Christianity exclude or minimize certain passages in the Bible and highlight other passages that support their views. They will often play the "interpretation" game when challenged with Bible passages that do not support their doctrine, or they may even redefine those passages as "spurious" or not really Scripture, or not relevant today.

Many of these groups will raise their historical extrabiblical beliefs and church practices to the level of Scripture. Some openly embrace this practice. Others deny it, but in practice affirm it. If you are part of a branded Christianity institution, look at where the institution's beliefs and practices are in light of the whole counsel of Scripture. For a start, look at the doctrines and/or practices on which the institution is unwilling to compromise (or those for which the institution criticizes others.)

And herein lies the problem. When we look at the attendance records of many of these institutions, even in countries with state-run churches, we find that only a small percentage of the population even attends church at all. In most cases, each brand of Christianity only draws from 2 to 5 percent, even in countries with state churches. Everyone who wants to go to a particular branded church is already attending one. Everyone else knows something about that brand of Christianity and chooses not to attend. In fact, many choose not to be a part of branded Christianity at all.

So, no matter what brand of Christianity is comfortable to you, it will only appeal to about 5 percent of the population at most. And everyone who is interested is already a member. Unfortunately, many of these members only attend on special occasions.

So, what makes us think that any one brand of Christianity, or even all that are working for the Great Commission, can succeed in reaching the world for Christ? Branded Christianity has been around for sixteen hundred years, and best-case numbers of those who call themselves Christian put us at 32 percent of the world's population.[2] And we know that only about 20 percent of those who call themselves Christians ever participate in any kind of church on a regular basis.[3]

If we keep doing what we have always done, we will keep getting the same results. Approaches promoted by branded Christian institutions for accomplishing the Great Commission have not succeeded in sixteen hundred years or in the years since the Protestant Reformation began in 1517. The reality is that Christianity does not have a good name in most of the world. We have made Christ like us, which is the vilest form of idolatry, instead of becoming like Christ. What makes us think that anyone wants our religion? They have seen it at work, and have rejected it. And the heart of Christian religion is those institutions that promote their own brand of Christianity.

Another barrier that results from branded Christianity is that leaders must go through extensive educational and indoctrination processes before they are qualified to lead. This bottleneck precludes any hope of completing the Great Commission before another generation dies. All the seminaries, Bible schools, and church networks combined cannot produce enough leaders to finish the task. The denominational education and indoctrination processes make it impossible to fulfill the Great Commission. We have come a long way from first-century, illiterate fishermen entering new people groups, nations, and cities and starting a church within months and then moving on. With the loss of simplicity we lost the ability to replicate leaders quickly and move through people groups efficiently. By overtraining and overmanaging new believers, we stop the process of replication that could reach a nation and a world.

Jesus left eleven men, some of whom doubted, standing on a hilltop. Some were illiterate. Others were rebels. All would be considered ill prepared to fulfill the task Christ gave to them and the church. If Christ deemed these eleven very marginal leaders fit enough to carry forward the Great Commission, perhaps we need to rethink what we are doing.

The DMM is about doing what was done in the first century—giving the Gospel to a people and teaching them to obey it; seeing them become faithful disciples of Christ; leaving them to struggle in obeying the Word of God in their own context and history; and allowing them to develop their own unique practices for worship, leadership, and governance within the confines of biblical obedience.

When institutions that promote a particular brand of Christianity forget their differences and get back to planting the Gospel instead of their doctrines, we may have a chance to complete the Great Commission. When we turn to making disciples of Christ instead of converts for our particular brand, we may have a chance to complete the Great Commission. Until then, Christians will be doomed to repeat the mistakes of our forefathers. Paul and I prefer to learn from our mistakes, not repeat them.

When institutions that promote branded Christianity begin to plant the Gospel, make obedient disciples of Christ, and forget their own pet doctrines and practices, we will see the Great Commission fulfilled in a generation. They will also see their own brand of Christianity grow as never before, because they will become relevant to the people as they serve them in obedience to the Word of God.

- Just because something is American or even "Christian" does that make it biblical? The truth of the matter is tradition and worldview creep up on us very quickly and they taint us. In order to share the gospel effectively we must strip these things away until scripture remains. The Holy Spirit transforms cultures beside the Bible.

DISCIPLE-MAKERS REALIZE THE STRUCTURE OF THE COMMUNITY DETERMINES THE STRATEGY USED TO MAKE DISCIPLES

Structure, strategy, and tactics are intimately related. In fact, structure determines strategy and tactics. If the objective is to capture a mountain, this objective determines the troops and equipment required. One wouldn't request wheeled vehicles to take a mountain. The vehicles would deliver well-trained ground troops to overcome the obstacles of the rugged terrain on foot.

Because structure determines strategy and tactics, one tool does not fit all situations. If an army has only tanks, it is limited to when and where tanks can operate. For this reason armies are varied and flexible in structure. Urban warriors are trained differently from desert warriors. Those who work at sea are trained differently from those who fly above the earth.

In recent articles about disciple-making, there is a lot of talk about structure. Debate rages between organic (house church) structures and institutional or traditional (megachurch) structures. There are churches structured around communities. Others are structured around programs. Still others focus on knowledge. Some like small groups. Others prefer worshipping in a large crowd of like believers. And some think all of this talk about structure is nonsense.

Most seminaries, Bible schools, and churches train their personnel to plant churches that mirror their own particular style or structure (brand). Megachurches plant more megachurches, or at least churches that should become megachurches. House churches plant only house churches and sometimes teach that all other structures are inadequate or even evil. When it comes to disciple-making, focusing on the structure of the sending church is like an army focusing on one kind of tool, or tactic, to take all objectives. Sometimes the army may be able to win because their limited structure and tactics are right for the objective. But most of the time it would be defeated. No matter how well trained, and no matter how motivated and committed they are to the mission, an army of tanks cannot take an objective that is made up of marshes, lakes, and rivers.

It is the structure of the objective that determines the strategy and tactics, not the structure of the tactic used to implement the strategy.

Unfortunately, the focus of most disciple-making has been on the structure of the church (the tool or tactic) that is doing the planting, not the community where the planting is to be done. If one is limited to the structure of the sending organization or church to start new churches, then the process is doomed to fail most of the time, because the people doing the work are focused on the structure of their tool, their tactics, instead of the structure of their objective.

An urban society is going to require different tactics from a rural society. A tribal culture is going to require different tactics from a nomadic one. The structures are different. Can one start a church using a building if the society is nomadic? Can one use democratic church polity if the society is tribal? Only by changing the structure of the society, which is a much more complicated and difficult task than starting an appropriately structured church, can one move people from their home structure to the structure of the church planter.

When I (David) went to India more than twenty years ago, a very wise worker said to me, "You can't change Indian culture; you have to fit into it." In the beginning I thought this was about my stress related to learning a new language and culture. Now I know it was about much more than how I talk, eat, or go to the bathroom.

The structure of church required to self-replicate in India is determined by Indian cultural and community structures, not by the structure of church with which I am comfortable. As a matter of fact, it is almost impossible for me to determine the structure that will work. My strategy, therefore, must be flexible and determined by what the local people require in order to continue functioning within their community structures.

This means that some places will require open-air congregations to grow and multiply. In other settings, small house groups may be required. In still other circumstances very organized building-based churches may be the best fit for the community.

Determining the structure of a community is called a *worldview study*. This instrument allows an outsider to get a good idea of the social and community structures before developing any tactics. Wise disciple-makers understand the objective and the strategy before putting tactics in place. Varied and diverse communities require varied and diverse tactics. These tactics are best when local workers are engaged in the strategy development process and at some point take the lead in strategy development.

Some have made the observation that Disciple-Making Movements have only been seen in rural societies. We think this is because rural societies are much less complex than urban societies, and just a few tactics are needed to start churches in these rural structures. When we look at the urban churches in our work, they are among village people who have moved to the city. So, basically, the same rural tactics are being used in the city and are reaching migrant populations, but not traditional urbanites. The traditional, premigration structures found in the urban setting will require us to develop new tactics.

This means the DMM-like disciple-making we have seen in some cities is really not DMM. It is a by-product of rural DMM methodologies that are working among rural peoples who have migrated to urban settings. There are few tactics in the urban setting that have been intentionally designed to start self-replicating churches in the varied communities of a megacity. These complex structures remain unaddressed by disciple-makers, and therefore we see slow-to-no growth in urban settings.

Megacities are extremely complex. There are literally thousands of community structures in a large city. No single tactic or small group of tactics is up to the task of reaching a major city. Disciple-making in a complex megacity will require thousands of tactics in order to be successful. Every kind of church known to man, plus more, will be required to meet the varied preferences of urban dwellers. We will have to allow new structures (communities) the privilege of coming up with new styles of church and worship if we are going to meet the needs of the postmodern and post-Christian city's troglodytes.

It is the structure of the community that determines the kind of church to be planted and the tactics to be used to reach the community. If you believe in only one brand of church, or if you are familiar with only a few different brands of church and allow these tool structures to determine your tactics, then you will fail more often than succeed in disciple-making. Success will be found in creative and intentional diversity of tactics and churches. This creativity will come from within the structures themselves, not from outsiders who have little understanding of the complex structures. (We will talk more about the difference between strategy and tactics when we discuss the practices of Contagious Disciple-Making.)

I have become all things to all
men so that by all possible means
I might save some. I do all this
for the sake of the gospel, that
I may share in its blessings.

—1 Corinthians 9:22-23

CHAPTER
6

DISCIPLE-MAKERS REALIZE THEIR CULTURE AND RELIGIOUS EXPERIENCE CAN NEGATIVELY INFLUENCE THEIR DISCIPLE-MAKING UNLESS THEY ARE VERY CAREFUL

There are thousands of kinds of churches, but there is only one Gospel. Certainly, the hope is that churches are based on the Gospel, but when a new church is started, what is the foundation? Is the foundation of the new church the church it came from—with all its cultural heritages—or is the foundation of the new church the Gospel of Jesus Christ?

Church has two major parts—the teachings of the Bible and the cultural expressions of obedience to these teachings that have developed over time and may have been borrowed from different cultures and times. Insiders in the church understand their culture without asking where it came from, but when we begin the process of disciple-making, we must not make our church culture the foundation for the new church, or it will fail. (By *fail*, we mean it will not naturally reproduce in the new context.)

When we focus on catalyzing Disciple-Making Movements, we define success by reproduction. We really don't care how many churches anyone has planted. If you tell me you have planted one hundred churches, my next question will be, "How many churches did the one hundred churches you planted start in the next year?" Success, for leadership, is defined by how many new leaders a leader reproduces every year.

In a recent training event I (David) asked the trainees, "Who are the people I am training?"

They looked around and replied, "Us."

I responded, "No, I am here to train your trainers."

Success is easy to spot. There will be four generations present. I will be present. The ones I am training will be present. The ones my trainees are training will be present. And the ones the trainees' trainees are training will be present.

We want to see four or more generations of leaders present, or we have failed. So, we say to leaders we work with, "Tell me about the people you are mentoring, and tell me about the people your mentees are mentoring." There is always an expectation of four generations, minimum. All good leaders are intimately aware of the two generations below them and the generation above them.

Back to disciple-making: culture is extremely difficult to pass on to others outside your culture because it requires people to leave behind, or lose, their own culture in order to adopt the new one. This is a barrier most people are unwilling to jump. Very few people want to be seen as different, and in some cultures no one does. This makes it difficult or impossible to start new churches if the foundation of the new church is a church culture from another time and place.

So, what kind of churches do we plant, anyway? We strive to plant the Gospel of Jesus Christ and let it transform individuals, families, and communities so that a culturally relevant and redeemed church will emerge. As we introduce the Gospel we

36

ask the question, "If this is from God, what are you going to do about it?" We insist that the role of any believer is to be obedient to the Gospel of Jesus Christ and allow it to redeem self, family, community, and culture.

As the new believers become obedient to the Gospel, worship emerges out of their culture and is acceptable to the culture within the limits set by God's Word. As they struggle with the Word, new leadership forms develop. As they strive with the new and push out that which is not from God, unique systems develop that look like the local culture but are redeemed by the Gospel. The church emerges out of obedience to the Word of God and expresses itself in uniquely cultural ways, thus removing or limiting the barriers of foreign culture and times.

Churches grow from the soil of culture where the seed of the Gospel is planted. This leads to churches that can naturally and quickly reproduce, as well as leaders who can reproduce. It makes disciples, who by the very definition of "disciple" reproduce more disciples.

In this model, everyone is trained to ask the question, "In this situation, how will I [or we] be obedient to the Word of God?" Faith is defined as the continuous act of choosing to be obedient to God's Word regardless of what it may cost, even our lives.

These are the kind of churches we see grow out of the Gospel we plant. They are obedient. They grow and they reproduce as a natural part of being and doing church. It starts slow, but exponentially reproduces very quickly. They become a Disciple-Making Movement.

CHAPTER
7

DISCIPLE-MAKERS UNDERSTAND THE IMPORTANCE OF OBEDIENCE

The Bible has a lot to say about obedience. As we look at our own lives, our churches, and the churches we've catalyzed, we recognize an ongoing struggle with obedience. The modern church has made the Christian life way too easy for its members. This has marginally increased the numbers attending our churches, but we're fairly certain it has caused many more problems than it solved. We have made salvation so easy that people can make their "profession of faith" or join the church and not change any behaviors that are disobedient or contrary to the Word of God. In our efforts to swell the ranks of the church, to be inclusive, to be politically correct, to impress others, we have thrown away one of the most important and foundational teachings of the Bible—obedience.

Jesus equated "obedience" to "love" in the Gospel of John, and John restated the principle in his first epistle:

- "If you love me, you will obey what I command." (John 14:15)

- "Whoever has my commands and obeys them, he is the one who loves me." (John 14:21)

- "He who does not love me will not obey my teaching." (John 14:24)

39

🌐 "This is love for God: to obey his commands. And his commands are not burdensome . . ." (1 John 5:3–4)

It is clear from the words of Jesus and the writings of John that there can be no love for Christ without obedience to Christ. We can sing all the worship songs ever written and proclaim to all that we love Christ, but these songs and statements are meaningless and hypocritical if we are not obedient to Him in every area of life. Our feelings do not define our love. Our words do not define our love. It is our motives, our actions, our obedience to Christ that define our love for Christ.

The Bible teaches that obedience to the commands and teachings of God has direct benefit to those who believe. Sometimes these benefits are to the corporate body of Christ. Other times the benefits are personal and individual. Deuteronomy 6:1–3 says:

> These are the commands, decrees and laws the LORD your God directed me to teach you to observe in the land that you are crossing the Jordan to possess, so that you, your children and their children after them may fear the LORD your God as long as you live by keeping all his decrees and commands that I give you, and so that you may enjoy long life. Hear, O Israel, and be careful to obey so that it may go well with you and that you may increase greatly in a land flowing with milk and honey, just as the LORD, the God of your fathers, promised you.

In the Old Testament, the blessings of obedience were often portrayed as corporate in nature. The result of teaching obedience is that subsequent generations would fear the Lord and the nation would enjoy long life, things would go well with the nation, and the nation would increase greatly in the land. Fear of the Lord is a choice to live in an awe, respect, honor, and reverence of the Creator God. This choice compels us to do exactly what the Lord says. These Old Testament passages speak volumes to the church. When we examine why our churches are not growing, we can easily say that the reason we are not increasing in the land is that we do not fear the Lord and do not teach our people to obey His laws, precepts, and commands. Notice that the object of teaching in the Great Commission and in the Deuteronomy passage is obedience, not the law. Most of us already know the law. We know what is right and wrong. But we have not been taught to obey what is right and avoid wrong regardless of personal consequence. Obedience requires us to do what is right even if we do not personally benefit or would be put at a disadvantage by obeying. The inconvenience of the individual believer when living in obedience is an advantage for the corporate body of believers, resulting in fear of the Lord, long life for the body, and increase in the number of members composing the body.

The following promises from God's Word can be taken corporately and individually:

> If you love me, you will obey what I command. And I will ask the Father, and he will give you another Counselor to be with you forever—the Spirit of truth. The world cannot accept him, because it neither sees him nor knows him. But you know him, for he lives with you and will be in you. I will not leave you as orphans; I will come to you. Before long, the world will not see me anymore, but you will see me. Because I live, you also will live. On that day you will realize that I am in my Father, and you are in me, and I am in you. Whoever has my commands and obeys them, he is the one who loves me. He who loves me will be loved by my Father, and I too will love him and show myself to him. (John 14:15–21)

This passage from the gospel of John gives us tremendous insights into the results of obedience for individuals and groups. Examine this list of benefits.

- Jesus will ask the Father to give us a Counselor (the Holy Spirit) who will be with us forever.

- The Holy Spirit will live with us and be in us.

- We will not be abandoned as orphans, but Christ will come to us.

- We will see Christ even if the world cannot see Him.

- We will live because Christ lives.

- We will be loved by the Father.

- We will be loved by Christ.

- Christ will show Himself to us.

We could write a book explaining these benefits alone, but Jesus was not finished.

> If anyone loves me, he will obey my teaching. My Father will love him, and we will come to him and make our home with him. He who does not love me will not obey my teaching. These words you hear are not my own; they belong to the Father who sent me. All this I have spoken while still with you. But the Counselor, the Holy Spirit, whom the Father will send in my name, will teach you all things and will remind you of everything I have said to you. (vv. 23–25)

Again, examine the benefits.

- The Father will love us.

- The Father and Christ will make their home with us.

- The Holy Spirit will teach us all things.

- The Holy Spirit will remind us of everything Christ has said.

But Jesus was not finished with obedience. Abiding in Christ is an obedience issue.

> I am the vine; you are the branches. If a man remains in me and I in him, he will bear much fruit; apart from me you can do nothing. If anyone does not remain in me, he is like a branch that is thrown away and withers; such branches are picked up, thrown into the fire and burned. If you remain in me and my words remain in you, ask whatever you wish, and it will be given you. This is to my Father's glory, that you bear much fruit, showing yourselves to be my disciples. (John 15:5–8)

The result of obedience (His words remain in us) is that Christ will abide in us. Again, look at the benefits.

- If we remain in Christ (obey Him), He remains in us.

- We will bear much fruit, showing ourselves to be His disciples.

- Our prayers will be answered (ask whatever you wish and it will be given to you).

He concluded:

> As the Father has loved me, so have I loved you. Now remain in my love. If you obey my commands, you will

remain in my love, just as I have obeyed my Father's commands and remain in his love. I have told you this so that my joy may be in you and that your joy may be complete. My command is this: Love each other as I have loved you. Greater love has no one than this, that he lay down his life for his friends. You are my friends if you do what I command. I no longer call you servants, because a servant does not know his master's business. Instead, I have called you friends, for everything that I learned from my Father I have made known to you. You did not choose me, but I chose you and appointed you to go and bear fruit—fruit that will last. Then the Father will give you whatever you ask in my name. This is my command: Love each other. (vv. 9–17)

Jesus tells us that in order to remain (abide) in His love, we must obey His commands. Look at these further benefits.

- Christ's joy will be in us.

- Our joy will be made complete.

- We are no longer servants, but friends of Christ.

- Everything that Christ knows will be made known to us.

- We are appointed to bear lasting fruit.

- The Father will give us whatever we ask for in the name of Christ.

By the way, asking "in the name of Christ" is not a formula, or a closing phrase for a prayer. To ask "in the name of Christ" means to ask from the position of being in Christ. To be in Christ can only be accomplished by obeying Christ. To ask "in the name of Christ" means we are in abiding relationship with

Christ through loving Him, and this love is demonstrated and proven by our obedience to everything He has commanded.

We receive one more insight from John in his first letter:

> Everyone who believes that Jesus is the Christ is born of God, and everyone who loves the father loves his child as well. This is how we know that we love the children of God: by loving God and carrying out his commands. This is love for God: to obey his commands. And his commands are not burdensome, for everyone born of God overcomes the world. This is the victory that has overcome the world, even our faith. (1 John 5:1–4)

Grace and mercy are God's love language to mankind. We receive grace and mercy from God. We cannot show God grace and mercy, so what is our love language to God? John says that our love for each other is a result of obedience to God's commands. Our love for God is defined by our obedience. In fact, it appears that God spells love o-b-e-y.

Our motives for being obedient determine if we are doing so out of love or out of legalism. If we obey God's commands to fit in with peers or to please those in authority, then we are bowing to legalism, whether it's a response to the rules of the group or our feeling that we can get something positive by behaving in an obedient fashion. Obedience motivated by love is not about any group. It's about Christ. This kind of love impacts all groups—family, school, work, and community.

The benefit of obedience, according to John, is that we will overcome the world. This means that through obedience we will overcome sin, and the things of the world will not defeat us. When we feel defeated by the world, our culture, our circumstances, it is most likely because we are not living in obedience to God's commands.

Jesus made it very clear that being His disciple is not easy: "Then he said to them all: 'If anyone would come after me, he must deny himself and take up his cross daily and follow me. For whoever wants to save his life will lose it, but whoever loses his life for me will save it. . . . And anyone who does not carry his cross and follow me cannot be my disciple'" (Luke 9:23–24; 14:27). The "cross" here is not a wayward son, an obnoxious spouse, a physical infirmity, or any other personal problem. The cross is an instrument of death. The impact of these statements is that those who want to be disciples of Jesus must be committed and ready to die, just as He died—on the cross. The commitment to follow Christ is not only a commitment to die to self, but also a commitment to be prepared to die for Christ and the world for which He died.

In the Great Commission Jesus commanded us to teach disciples to obey: "Then Jesus came to them and said, 'All authority in heaven and on earth has been given to me. Therefore go and make disciples of all nations, baptizing them in the name of the Father and of the Son and of the Holy Spirit, and teaching them to obey everything I have commanded you. And surely I am with you always, to the very end of the age'" (Matt. 28:18–20). In reality we have been teaching knowledge, not obedience. Most people already know what they are supposed to do, but they choose not to do it.

There are, of course, times when Satan will try to deceive us into thinking we are not living in obedience. This results in a false guilt that can rob us of our joy and our relationships. We must be diligent in examining times of guilt. If the Holy Spirit does not bring to mind the exact event where we have been disobedient, then we are experiencing false guilt from Satan, who is trying to steal our joy, kill our relationships with God, and destroy our love for Christ and His disciples.

DISCIPLE-MAKERS MAKE DISCIPLES, NOT CONVERTS

A *disciple* is one who embraces and obeys all the teachings of Christ and endeavors by word and deed to make more disciples. A *convert* is one who practices a religion into which he or she was not born, and may or may not encourage others to convert. Jesus commanded us to "go and make disciples of all nations, baptizing them in the name of the Father and of the Son and of the Holy Spirit, and teaching them to obey everything" He has commanded us (Matt. 28:19–20).

Jesus also condemned the making of converts: "Woe to you, teachers of the law and Pharisees, you hypocrites! You travel over land and sea to win a single convert, and when he becomes one, you make him twice as much a son of hell as you are" (Matt. 23:15).

There is a third group—those who were born in a Christian family and may profess Christ, but pick and choose which of His teachings they will follow. We treat this last category as if they were lost. First John 3:4–6 says, "Everyone who sins breaks the law; in fact, sin is lawlessness. But you know that he appeared so that he might take away our sins. And in him is no sin. No one who lives in him keeps on sinning. No one who continues to sin has either seen him or known him."

Jesus said, "If your brother sins against you, go and show him his fault, just between the two of you. If he listens to you, you have won your brother over. But if he will not listen, take one or two others along, so that 'every matter may be established by the testimony of two or three witnesses.' If he refuses to listen to them, tell it to the church; and if he refuses to listen even to the church, treat him as you would a pagan or a tax collector" (Matt. 18:15–17).

Making disciples is about having a relationship with Christ that results in a lifestyle of obedience to Christ's commands, which requires disciples to make more disciples. Making converts is about adhering to the doctrine of a particular faction, church, denomination, sect, or religion. One can convert without becoming a disciple of Christ. Subsequent-generation Christians are more like converts than disciples if they were not made disciples during their childhood and youth by consistently obedient parents and/or other significant adults.

In our experience, Contagious Disciple-Makers focus on helping people come into a dynamic and growing relationship with Christ through prayer, Bible study, worship, evangelism, fellowship, and ministry. Disciple-makers first teach people the Word of God so they will know what to obey. Second, they train people in the skill sets necessary to be an obedient follower of Christ so they will know how to obey. And third, disciple-makers equip people to their full capacity to serve God and others so they demonstrate lives of consistent obedience and make more disciples.

Often, those of us responsible for making disciples stop short in our disciple-making. We teach and train, but go no further. Demonstration of the knowledge and the skill sets are all we seem to value. Equipping requires us to be in relationship with those we are discipling. In equipping, we engage in more than just classroom or teaching/training time. The equipper and the equipped become a part of each other's lives. Part of the reason we don't see more of the equipping discipleship model that Jesus demonstrated with His life is that for it to work, we have to be absolutely consistent in public and private. The ones we are discipling should be able to drop in on us at any time and find us faithful and obedient to all the teachings of Christ. Many of us do not want to be under this kind of scrutiny or accountability, so we avoid making disciples, and instead make students or trainees. We are committed to teaching classes or holding training events, where we only have to look good for a relatively brief period of time.

Please note that it requires no faith to learn something. It requires no faith to teach or to train someone else. But discipleship requires faith: the faith to be a believer in and a follower of Christ, and the faith to do what Christ commands—the faith to say to others, "If you want to be a disciple of Christ, copy my life" (see 1 Corinthians 4:16; Philippians 4:9; and 1 Timothy 4:12). Learning does not require faith, just intellect. Obedience requires faith. It is a faith that, when acted out, says to others, "I will obey all the commands of Christ regardless of the circumstances in which I find myself or the consequences of any actions I must take or the consequences of any words I must say in order to be obedient to Christ in all matters, public and private."

The primary characteristic of a disciple is change demonstrated by a growth in character that requires increasing knowledge, appropriate attitudes, right thoughts, improving relationships, and obedient action. Christ does not change. He is perfect. The disciple's responsibility is to become like Christ. Change happens as a disciple strives to be like his Master. A disciple constantly struggles for perfection. When he misses or falls short of the mark (the root meaning of *amartia* [*hamartia*], Greek for "sin," is to fall short of or miss the target), he repents and aims for and moves toward the target again. The target is to be like Christ in all things, including knowledge, attitudes, thoughts, relationships and actions. Jesus said, "Be perfect, therefore, as your heavenly Father is perfect" (Matt. 5:48).

Perfection appears to be an impossible goal, but it must be our goal nonetheless. Even though Christ is our righteousness through faith, we must make every effort to be like Him in every way. Jesus said, "If anyone would come after me, he must deny himself and take up his cross daily and follow me. For whoever wants to save his life will lose it, but whoever loses his life for me will save it. What good is it for a man to gain the whole world, and yet lose or forfeit his very self?" (Luke 9:23–25).

DISCIPLE-MAKERS UNDERSTAND THE IMPORTANCE OF THE PRIESTHOOD OF THE BELIEVER

The doctrine of the Priesthood of Believers is incredibly important to disciple-making. It affirms the work of the Holy Spirit in the lives of all believers; it affirms the ministry potential and responsibility of all believers; and it empowers all believers to function as needed for the church to minister to the people who are not a part of the body of Christ as well as those who are part of the body of Christ.

This one doctrine opens the door and fuels the passion for any believer to be an apostle, prophet, evangelist (better understood as disciple-maker), and pastor/teacher. It moves Christianity from a profession to a lifestyle. It empowers the ordinary to do the extraordinary. It makes the church relevant and essential to a healthy community. And it appears that much of the modern church is throwing this doctrine out the door.

In place of the doctrine of the priesthood of all believers, we now see a strengthening of the priesthood of the pastor only. Somehow, all the ministry of the church has been focused in one position, even though the Bible is clear that there are multiple leadership roles, and the role of pastor is not the greatest of these roles, but one among many leadership roles in the church, both local and global.

The very teachings that attempt to strengthen the role of the pastor and promote it to a superior or exclusive leadership role are detrimental to the mandate to reach the nations for Christ. In an effort to strengthen the authority of pastoral leadership, the church has weakened the responsibility of all believers to function as priests. Professional leadership in the church has resulted in a reduction of those who feel qualified to minister. The net result is a weaker church, one that does not have the infrastructure to multiply, expand, or grow. Instead of protecting the church, these teachings that focus on the exclusive leadership role of the pastor have damaged the church.

Scripture makes it clear that the role of leadership in the church is to equip the Saints (believers) for the works of ministry (Eph. 4:11–13). Leaders are to be servants, not rulers (Luke 22:24–27). Leaders are to be examples in public and private, not authority figures (1 Tim. 4:11–13; Titus 2:6–8; 1 Peter 5:1–3). Only the leaders who serve and fulfill their commitments to equip the Saints are worthy of honor, worthy of the responsibility to lead, and worthy to be the ones we follow (1 Tim. 5:17–21). Position is a result of fulfilling the servant-leader role, not a result of going to school, having a degree, being ordained, or being called "pastor."

By promoting and insisting on a professional clergy, the church has limited its ability and capacity to reach the world for Christ. We have made it impossible to rapidly expand the church because we cannot produce enough "qualified" leaders to meet the expansion needs. We find so-called leaders who object to new Bible study groups, emerging leaders, and new churches in their areas because they feel threatened, instead of being excited that the lost are being engaged. The more the role of pastor is highlighted and strengthened by mandate rather than service, the less effective the role will become, and the less relevant it will be in reaching the world for Christ.

We must never forget that Jesus died for the lost. He told us to leave behind the ninety-nine sheep in the pen to find the one that is lost (Luke 15:3–7). We have become so concerned with protecting the pens that we forget that a primary role is to find the lost. It is the job of the leadership of the church to equip church members to fulfill this role.

The role of pastor should be to equip the Saints to obey all the commands of Christ. The pastor should be a champion of evangelism and disciple-making. He needs to encourage people to start and facilitate new groups, teach, witness, baptize new believers, serve the Lord's Supper, and minister to the needs of the community and the body of Christ. The pastor should be equipping his people for every ministry in life and pushing them out into the lost world to make a difference rather than locking them behind the doors of contrived doctrines designed to weaken the believer.

In many ways our churches are becoming jails. Jails are designed to isolate from society those who would harm it. Many churches now seem to be designed to isolate Christians from society so they cannot transform it.

Those who should be leading our churches are the men and women who have demonstrated their love and service, and have established a ministry of equipping the Saints for the works of ministry. When we find men and women doing this, we should call them out, equip them further, and pay them full-time so they can devote themselves to the ministry of the Gospel and the equipping of the Saints. (Please note: People like this are being paid so they do not have to work additional jobs to provide for themselves and their families. Their contribution to the body of Christ is so critical that allowing them to spend time away from serving the body of Christ to provide for their families would be a waste of time and resources. Not everyone will fit this criterion, and that is okay. People who don't fit it should probably not be paid to leave their jobs and become full-time ministers.) The qualification to become a pastor or any other leader in the church should be simply, is he or she living the life of a servant-leader? Unless one is serving, that person should not be given the opportunity to train and lead. To call men and women to be our leaders should be a response to their service, their equipping of others, and their success in personal and corporate ministry.

Herein lies the problem: Our current system of leadership does not promote obedient leaders who serve, are identified as servant leaders, and are then requested to give up their lives outside of full-time ministry to adopt a life of equipping the Saints. We have a broken system of discovering who is truly a called and gifted leader. Leaders grow by reproducing leaders. Our current systems are not designed to produce leaders, and part of the result of these systems is that few leaders excel— that is, produce more leaders for kingdom work by equipping the Saints for ministry.

In our current system, those who can break this chain of ignorance and failure are the local pastor and other responsible leaders. When the local pastor moves from being a ruler to a servant, from being an office holder to being an active servant-leader, from being the holder of knowledge to the trainer of disciples, from being the protector of orthodoxy to the motivator of obedient followers of Christ, and from focusing on all the church does to projecting who Christ is within communities, we will see a change in the church and the impact it has on individuals, communities, nations, and the world.

Pastors and their staffs must stop keeping their congregations as infants in the Word and ministry by doing everything for them. For congregations to mature and leaders to emerge, the pastor must treat his congregation as capable to serve and train them to serve. When pastors exhort and help their people become successful in obeying Christ's commands, their authority will grow, their honor will increase, and the Kingdom will benefit.

We will not see the world reached for Christ in any generation as long as leaders are protecting their fiefdoms instead of being about the King's business. We have been commanded to teach them to obey. We have been commanded to equip the Saints. We have been commanded to offer ourselves as living sacrifices. We have been commanded to be an example to the saved and lost alike. When we who call ourselves pastors and leaders start obeying, our churches will change, our communities will be transformed, and just maybe, we will see the world come to Christ in our generation.

PRACTICES OF A
DISCIPLE-MAKER

THINKING STRATEGICALLY AND TACTICALLY ABOUT DISCIPLE-MAKING

(Paul) have been to so many conferences and heard young hotshot pastors talk about their success. Their stories are usually variations of, "I was young and moved into a difficult neighborhood, full of ideas on how I was going to bring Jesus into that space. None of my ideas worked. I decided to scrap my plan and just love and serve the community. Pretty soon we had more people coming than we could handle." Usually, the young leader wrote a book, and many conference attendees bought it. The book contained ideas the author called "principles" or "strategies."

Over the next year, conference attendees would try to apply what they had heard and read, with limited success in their context. More than likely, they would then go to another conference to hear another speaker and purchase another book. Or, they might throw everything aside, stumble into success, reverse engineer the process, and write a book of their own. Many, though, live in a constant state of frustration, wondering what they did wrong.

There is nothing wrong with conferences and speakers. What confuses potential disciple-makers and church planters is the way many speakers and authors handle concepts like "strategy" and "tactics." Clearly defining these concepts helps us as we talk about what needs to happen to make disciples in our neighborhoods. Understanding these terms allows us to evaluate books we read and the speakers we hear to determine if their ideas will help us in our context, or work against us.

Strategy addresses the question, "What will it take to . . . ?" For me, I make this strategy question more specific to my context: "What will it take to catalyze Disciple-Making Movements in every community in the Pacific Northwest?". As you can tell, this question goes far beyond what I, or my organization, can do alone. In fact, answering this question with an "I" statement like, "I will go door-to-door and . . . ," means I'm not thinking broadly enough. The strategy question forces us to consider the big picture and evaluate the major elements that must be present to fulfill the vision.

When David started the work among the Bhojpuri, he asked the strategy question. One of the answers was deceptively simple. In fact, it was so simple it could be expressed in one word: "Scripture." Now, in those days, there was no written Bhojpuri language. Consequently, there were no Bhojpuri Bibles. Furthermore, many Bhojpuri were illiterate. But, David knew the Bhojpuri needed a Bible in their own language and in a format—audio—they would use. So he began the ten-year process of finding people to work on putting the Bhojpuri language in a written format, so they could translate the Bible into Bhojpuri, find a partner to help make a Bhojpuri audio Bible, and make disciples among the people of that region.

The results were amazing. One year they distributed one thousand audio Bibles. By the end of the year, there were more than six hundred churches planted as a direct result of those audio Bibles.

David knew he would not make disciples among Bhojpuri speakers if he didn't have Scripture. Without Scripture, everything would fall apart. This illustrates an important point: If something is truly strategic, then without it in place the plan will fail. If the plan can survive without an element, that element isn't strategic.

Being a disciple who makes disciples, prayer, engagement, Persons of Peace, Discovery Groups, establishing churches, and leadership development are all strategic. Each is part of the answer to the question, "What will it take to catalyze Disciple-Making Movements?" (There are others, but this book focuses on the strategic elements you need to get a movement started.) If you remove any of these elements, you won't have a movement, period. You may have some growth, but you won't experience movement.

Tactics, on the other hand, answer the question, "What must I, or my team, do to . . . ?" In the case of catalyzing Disciple-Making Movements, the questions are:

- What must I, or my team, do to be a disciple who makes disciples?

- What must I, or my team, do to pray and mobilize prayer?

- What must I, or my team, do to engage tribes of lost people?

- What must I, or my team, do to find Persons of Peace?

- What must I, or my team, do to start Discovery Groups?

- What must I, or my team, do to help new believers establish churches?

- What must I, or my team, do to help identify and develop emerging leaders?

Tactical answers focus on what you and your team will do to implement a strategic element. The tactical question based on prayer is, "What will I (and/or my team) do to pray for our neighborhood and mobilize prayer for our neighborhood?" As you will learn from the chapter on prayer, you can start a prayer calendar, schedule a prayer walk, and organize a small prayer gathering. You might even use tools like Facebook and Twitter to communicate with your prayer network.

Unlike strategic elements, you can remove a tactic from your plan and still fulfill the vision. If I didn't use Facebook, my plan to mobilize prayer wouldn't fall apart. I'd do something else. If I'm in a country where people don't use Facebook, then obviously I'm going to choose a different tactic. Tactics are flexible. They change with the personalities and skill of the people on your team. They also change with the limitations and challenges of the environment.

Understanding the relationship between vision, strategy, and tactics helps with leading teams of highly-driven, called, and talented people. The team sticks to the vision and the strategy. The tactics, however, can change from person to person, as long as they don't contradict the strategy. Again, looking at prayer, each team member can select a different way to mobilize prayer support, and personal goals for mobilizing support. After an agreed-upon period, the team comes back and reviews each tactic and goals. Keep tactics that work; reevaluate tactics that didn't work as you thought they should; get rid of tactics that fail.

A word of caution: Too many people get married to their tactics and forget that tactics serve the strategy. Consequently, they don't know what to do when their tactic isn't working. They may get angry or defensive when people try to suggest different tactics. Keep tactics in perspective. Set up regular reviews.

Dispose of tactics that aren't working for you. Keep your ego away from your tactics.

The remainder of this book deals with the main strategic elements necessary to be a Contagious Disciple-Maker and to catalyze Disciple-Making Movements. We will provide many examples and stories of how teams in the United States and around the globe used various tactics to implement these strategic elements in their communities. Our hope is that you will have a good understanding of each strategic element and an idea of some tactics used by others. Some of the tactics will work in your community. Many will not. Implementation and evaluation are up to you and your team. You will try many things and discover which tactics work for you. Have fun, and don't be afraid of failure.

BE A DISCIPLE WHO MAKES DISCIPLES

The fall in Genesis 3 started humankind down a path that still impacts all of us. God gave Adam and Eve a very simple command. In Genesis 2:16–17, "the LORD God commanded man, saying, 'From any tree of the garden you may eat freely; but from the tree of the knowledge of good and evil you shall not eat, for in the day that you eat from it you will surely die'" (NASB). Satan responded to this command in Genesis 3:4–5, "You surely will not die! For God knows that in the day you eat from it your eyes will be opened, and you will be like God, knowing good and evil" (NASB). In verse 6 the greatest dilemma of man is birthed: "When the woman saw that the tree was good for food, and that it was a delight to the eyes, and that the tree was desirable to make one wise, she took from its fruit and ate; and she gave also to her husband with her, and he ate" (NASB).

God gave Adam and Eve one command—don't eat from the tree in the middle of the garden. He expected them to obey. Satan countered God's command with the illusion that knowledge of good and evil will make one like God, and this is better than obedience. Eve interpreted this to mean that the fruit would make her wise. The search for knowledge and wisdom has persistently plagued humanity, as God later said, "Anyone who loves me will obey my teaching" (John 14:23).

When we examine the many discipleship systems available, most are knowledge-based rather than obedience-based. The commands God gave us are there to keep us from harm. We understand that knowledge is essential to obedience. But knowledge without obedience seems to be the fruit that the church and many who call themselves Christian continue to eat.

God's commands are not designed to restrict life or happiness; they are designed to preserve life and happiness by warning us of the emotional, spiritual, and social minefields found in a fallen and imperfect world. God's commands are warning signs that, when obeyed, make life safer, better, and more productive. Any moral command of God is there to keep us from hurting our families, our societies, and ourselves. Let's sample a few.

Do not murder. Murder destroys individuals and families, degrades society, and puts the murderer and the one murdered into a position of suffering eternal consequences for the action. There is more than one victim in any murder. Even the murderer is a victim of his or her own sin.

Do not commit adultery. Adultery destroys families, has significant financial impact on society, degrades all relationships, and certainly negatively impacts the future of those involved in the onerous relationship.

Do not steal. Stealing disrupts, and sometimes destroys, the lives of the victims, and pollutes the lives of the perpetrators. The thief lives in constant dread of being discovered, or grows so callous that other people's lives have no meaning. Stealing destroys the economy and destroys families and societies. Our cost of living would go down significantly if there were an end to theft in all its forms.

Do not get drunk. This is not about drinking alcoholic beverages; it's about losing control of your behavior due to excessive drinking and letting your lack of inhibition get you into trouble. Ask the families of those who have been killed by drunk drivers, or the families of convicted drunk drivers who have lost their freedom, their savings to legal bills and lawsuit settlements, their incomes, and their self-esteem. Ask the drunks and their families how it feels to be homeless, poor, or abused. There is no victimless disobedience of God's commands.

Think of others as better than yourself. On the surface this looks like a mild problem, but in reality, disobeying this command is one of the most destructive behaviors in any society. When a person puts all others behind herself in all decision making and in all behaviors, it results in a total breakdown of personal relationships, families, and societies. This form of pride puts us center stage, and the whole world exists for our pleasure, regardless of how it impacts others. Just take a look at any despot and the countries he has ruined, and you will see the results of disobeying this command; or take a look at any family where one person rules and all others exist to make her happy, when in fact there is no happiness in such families for anyone.

Do not have sex outside of marriage. The health costs alone make this one important, not to mention the pain and guilt as well as the negative relationship consequences a few minutes of self-indulgence in illicit sex will bring.

Just like an activated mine, every broken command of God triggers destruction. Please note that it is our actions doing the destruction, not God. God loves us and wants us to avoid the minefields of life and the destruction they bring. He has instructed us regarding all the risks in life that will impact our families, our societies, and us. There will always be those who will plant minefields. There will always be those who love the thrill of tiptoeing through the minefields. And there will always be those who will seek or cause destruction by encouraging people to enter the minefields, known or unknown.

Only a fool would disregard a minefield sign. No one willingly passes through a minefield, especially when there is a warning of its existence. Yet every day there are billions of people who disregard the Bible's warnings, which are designed to help us avoid the minefields of life.

The problem with mines is that they do not only injure or kill the person or vehicle full of people that triggers the mine. An activated mine has a destructive radius that immediately impacts not only the people inside the circle of destruction but also all who know them, and even those who don't know them but see them being mangled or destroyed by the mine. One mine can change the lives of hundreds of people in a flash.

God's commands are the warning signs that help lessen the impact of those who would destroy us. His demand for obedience is meant not to make us miserable but to preserve the lives and health of our families, our societies, and ourselves. The next time you are tempted to disobey God, think of the consequences, and then just don't do it. Heed the warning signs, turn around, and go another way.

The path to consistent obedience requires a great deal of discipline. Knowledge alone will not get one there. God knows this, and early in His relationship with His people, He instructed Moses to write the following:

> Hear, O Israel: The LORD our God, the LORD is one. Love the LORD your God with all your heart and with all your soul and with all your strength. These commandments that I give you today are to be on your hearts. Impress them on your children. Talk about them when you sit at home and when you walk along the road, when you lie down and when you get up. Tie them as symbols on your hands and bind them on your foreheads. Write them on the doorframes of your houses and on your gates. (Deut. 6:4–9)

The passage opens with the Hebrew word *Shamah*, which can be translated as "hear," "observe," or "obey." The intent of the word is for us to "hear and obey" the rest of this passage.

We must understand that there is only one God and He is our Lord. And what follows helps us understand how we connect to Him. We must love Him with all our hearts and all our souls and all our strength.

Even during the time of Moses, the heart was considered the center of emotion. Our love for God is to have passion. This is the origin of worship. It is in our passion for God that our prayer lives develop. This is where we get that feeling-good-about-our-relationship-with-God sensation. Sometimes we go to worship and don't feel good about it. There are other times we walk into worship and—wow! It just blows us over. Our emotional side can come and go. We certainly have difficulty getting excited about every worship service, and there are times we don't even start feeling anything related to worship until we're halfway home.

"Love the Lord your God . . . with all your heart." The word "all" means all, and that's all it means! If you have reserved stuff in your heart for other things besides God, you're not going to experience the depth in relationship you desire. In Psalm 90 Moses wrote about secret sin—sin that we hide from everyone, but which God sees. We've reserved that part of our heart for the things that we like to do in sin. We all struggle with this.

We know we struggle. There are things we like to do that we know we shouldn't. Combined, Paul and I have been following Christ for more than eighty years. Even then, we admit that sometimes we think, *You know, I'd really like to do that, but somebody might see me* or *I'm not going to say this because somebody might hear me.* It's in our hearts, and we struggle with it. The longer we wrestle without the intent to conquer that battle, the less we experience God's presence in our lives because we've reserved part of our hearts for something or someone else. All means all, and that's all it means. Anything less and we miss what God has for us.

"Love the Lord your God . . . with all your soul." If we asked you to send us a paragraph defining "soul," we'd probably receive a different answer from each reader. But let's see if we can put together something we can all agree on. We're sure you could add to the following, but we are looking for what would bring us all together, not what would divide us.

The soul is eternal. It is individually identifiable for eternity. The soul doesn't move around in circles of reincarnation, and it doesn't change from person to person. It's one soul for one life, for one person, forever.

So here's the picture. Love the Lord with that part of you that's eternal. If you've invested in God for eternity, you'll look at life differently. He says, "I want you to love Me with that part of you that's eternal so you will know beyond a doubt that you are connected to Me." It's that forever connectedness at the soul level that gets you through disaster points in your life that you don't think you can live through. If you haven't been through any of those yet, just wait a while and they will catch up to you. If your love for God does not connect at the soul level, then when you hit the wall of disaster in your life, you won't have anything to take you through it. Then suddenly "it's God's fault; He's doing this to me," and you start asking all kinds of questions about who God is and what His place is in your life.

If there's love in that eternal part of our lives, we recognize that our promise is eternity and beyond just the now. A lot of now has to be lived out in the kingdom of Satan, not in the Kingdom of God. The kingdom of Satan wants to destroy us. We have to learn how to deal with Satan's kingdom even though we are a part of God's Kingdom. We live in the world, the kingdom of Satan. It's going to have trash in it, crap in it, hell in it, but these are things you have to deal with. You don't know from one minute to the next what's going to happen.

Recently a friend called me (David), and through his tears he said, "My daughter was just killed by a drunk driver." This leader of a strong Christian family asked, "Why did God let this happen?" There is no way to console anyone at that point. I said, "Please be assured, God is with you, and we'll talk about this later, but right now I'm coming over just to sit with you." I knew that if I could help him through his grief, a time would come when we could talk about his questions. Right then he was not at a place where he could hear the truth. So, I just let him know that God's love transcends these events and our understanding. It is loving God with all our souls that gets us through these encounters.

"Love the Lord your God . . . with all your strength." This is a common metaphor that refers to our actions. Everything we do is to demonstrate to others that we love God. Colossians 3:23–24 says, "Whatever you do, do your work heartily, as for the Lord rather than for men, knowing that from the Lord you will receive the reward of the inheritance. It is the Lord Christ whom you serve" (NASB).

"These commandments that I give you today are to be on your hearts." This is a new metaphor. Even in the day of Moses people knew that life ended when the heart stopped beating.

This metaphor puts the commands of God as the life-giving heart of mankind. And in the same way we don't think about our hearts beating, we should not have to think about obeying the commands of God.

A few years back I had heart bypass surgery. When I woke up in recovery with all that equipment—the ventilator, IVs, drain tubes, and more—the one thing I noticed was that I could hear my heart beating. I'm not talking about the *beep . . . beep . . . beep* on the cardiac monitor. I could audibly hear my heart beating! A few days later they moved me into a regular room, and I could still hear my heart beating. I asked the surgeon, "Why am I hearing my heart beat?" He laughed and said, "When we did surgery on your heart, we changed its sound, and your brain hasn't gotten used to the new sound of your heart yet. So, until your brain begins to filter the sound of your heart, you're going to hear it." It was really comforting the first few days, but after day six it was a little old! *Thump-thump, thump-thump, thump-thump . . .* I was ready to pull my hair out; I was hearing my heart all the time!

Then one morning I woke up and didn't hear my heart, and thought, *Oh no!* I looked up, and the monitor was doing its number. I told the doctor and he just laughed! He says it happens to everyone. Our brains develop a filter that neutralizes the sound of our hearts; otherwise we would always hear them. It's a very noisy, rhythmic system.

These laws, these decrees that God has given, are to be so automatic in our lives that we don't have to think about them. Obedience is not something we have to think about doing; it just happens—like our hearts beating.

"Impress them on your children. Talk about them when you sit at home and when you walk along the road, when you lie down and when you get up." In this verse Moses begins to tell us how to develop a love for God and an obedience that is automatic.

How do we become so autonomic in our obedience that we don't even have to think about being obedient? Moses used the word "impress." The English word *impress* is the same word used when a coin is minted. My father was a coin collector and had a coin from the time of Jesus. It had a recognizable image of

Caesar. I visited a mint, and part of the tour took us where they were making coins. I asked, "How much pressure is required to imprint that image on the coin?" The reply was fifty tons done twice for each side of the coin. I asked, "How long will the image last?" The guide said, "Unless the molecular integrity of the metal is destroyed with high heat, that image will always be there. Even if you couldn't see it, I could put it under an electron microscope and you could still see the crystallization from the impression in the metal itself." The image impressed on a coin really is as eternal as humans can make it.

Moses commanded us to impress God's love and His commandments upon our children, both physical and spiritual. "Talk about them [referring to the laws, the commands, the decrees of the Lord] when you sit at home and when you walk along the road and when you lie down and when you get up."

Here's the picture. What we think, say, and do at home should be the same as what we think, say, and do when we're away. What we think, say, and do during the most intimate moments with family and what we think, say and do during the moments that are not intimate should be the very same. There's a consistency of living in public and in private, in intimate and non-intimate moments. Our character stays the same regardless of our situation. Our response to stress and to other people stays the same. It is living a consistent life that impresses on another human being the importance of knowing the Lord and living in this kind of relationship with Him.

Over the years we have worked with wayward MKs (missionary kids) who had dropped out of school, been sent to jail for drugs, and found themselves in all kinds of trouble. As we began to work with these young men, we noticed a pattern— their parents were not the same people at home as they were in public. They would say one thing in public and live another life at home. They would say in front of others, "Don't watch R-rated movies," but they'd have a whole library of R-rated movies at home—and sometimes worse than that. They'd say, "Love your neighbor" while in public, and then come home and yell and scream about everything. There was this dichotomy of public life and private life in the history of every one of these young MKs. You have to live a life that is absolutely consistent.

My wife and I recently got a satellite TV system at our house. The first thing we did was go to parental controls and block out all the channels and movies with ratings that we knew we shouldn't watch. When we entered in the code that blocked them, my wife put in the first two numbers and I put in the second two numbers, and we were done. I don't even remember the two numbers I put in, and I'm sure she doesn't remember her two numbers. But we didn't want to be surfing channels and see something we didn't want to see. And we certainly didn't want guests coming to our house, surfing through the channels, and hitting something that would shock them and bring into question our values. This is part of my family's obedience; we try to be consistent in what we say to people. If you look at our books, our movies, or anything in our house, the values they represent are consistent with the life we say we live.

One of the aspects of mentoring we teach is for the mentor to spend time in the homes of mentees, and for mentees to spend time in the homes of their mentors. When you stay in someone's home for more than a few days, he can't hide from you how he's living, particularly if there are kids in the house.

Consistency. Absolute consistency is required if you want to impress God's love and commands on your physical and spiritual children.

"Tie them as symbols on your hands and bind them on your foreheads. Write them on the doorframes of your houses and on

your gates." Often when we don't want to obey something, we turn it into a symbol, but this admonition of Moses' is a little bit more than just symbolism. Something written on your forehead is for others to see, not you. Communicate to your culture that you are sold out 100 percent to God. In the Jewish context, God's people put the phylactery (a small square box, made of leather, that contained scriptures written on small pieces of paper) on as a reminder that they were totally devoted to God. How do you, in your culture, demonstrate that you belong to God? This would be how you "bind it on your forehead."

"Tie them as symbols on your hands" refers to personal reminders about your identity and your behavior. At 9:00 every morning there's a pop-up on my iPhone that says, "Have you done your Bible study?" I have a 24/7 ministry. People contact me at every hour of the day. How do I keep track of all I do, as well as my Bible study? Some days I start at three o'clock in the morning with a conference call, and before I know it I've blown through the whole day without spending time in the Word. So, I have to have reminders about Bible reading, study, and prayer times.

When I work, I'm usually a highly focused person. In fact, I get so focused that sometimes the whole day will go by and my wife will come to me and say, "Do you realize you missed lunch and dinner?" I say no, and she says, "I knew you didn't." So, I have reminders to get up and move around so I don't sit too long. The point is, I have reminders in my life. One reminder my wife and I have is to ask each other, "What have you learned today in your Bible study?"

What reminders do you have in your life to help you love God with all your heart, soul, and strength? These have to be active reminders. My wife and I tried hanging scriptures on the wall, but this became just like anything else on the wall; we got used to it. What active reminders do you have to poke and remind you, *Are you being who you're supposed to be? Are you practicing the things you're supposed to practice? Are you living out the things you say you live out?* Do you even have reminders?

Part of the mentor's responsibility is to be an active reminder to the mentee of the things she's supposed to be doing and being in her relationship to God, to her family, to her community and church, to her call, to her job, and to herself. The mentor/mentee relationship is an active reminder about who we're supposed to be. When you're a true mentor, every question you ask is fair game for the mentee to ask you. It's never a one-way street when you're a mentor. It's a two-way street. It's an active learning process going both directions.

The Hebrew home was designed to be like the tabernacle. Who sees the gates? Everyone. Who sees the doorposts? Family, friends, and guests. What the visitor sees from the outside is what he gets on the inside. The writing on the gate and the doorframe really do represent the sentiments and actions of the home. The declaration of who you are really is who you are. This consistency impresses our God onto the lives of our children.

Many of us wear masks. We tend to avoid identifying ourselves as highly spiritual people to the public. The result is that no one ever comes through our doors seeking to know why we are so spiritual. As you begin to self-identify as a highly spiritual person by being publicly, conspicuously spiritual, you'll start to see people who want spiritual lives coming through the gate to see if your spirituality is true. They come inside your lives and see that it is true. This is a part of engaging and reaching those who don't know God and don't want to know our God. It's a part of reaching our neighborhoods, cities, nation, and world. We have to be consistent in public and in private.

The entire picture of this passage is that if we are not who we're supposed to be all the time, then God will not use us to bring the Gospel to others. I know that there are some exceptions to that rule, that there are some real scoundrels spreading the Gospel, but in obedience to the Word of God, our responsibility is to live conspicuous, consistent, spiritual lives that are open to examination at any time, under any circumstances, by other people.

When I look at the times when my ministry has accelerated, it's been during periods of extreme spiritual stress. More people came to Christ in Asia when my father died than before. They watched me deal with the event. They watched how I dealt with my family, how I dealt with my children, how I dealt with outsiders, how I closed down my father's business; they watched everything. People started coming to me with a common statement: "We don't know how you did that, but we would like to know how."

They saw something that they could not do spiritually or emotionally or physically. And because of that event, when we got expelled from the country, more people came to know Christ. When we got expelled from the next country, the same thing happened. They witnessed those high-stress moments when we had fear, anger, and frustration, but appropriately talked through those emotions rather than acting out. And when we made mistakes, our apologies had power because they were a part of a consistent life. These life events cry out, *I am the person I am asking you to be.*

One of my favorite lines from the apostle Paul is, "You want to know how to be a Christian? Look at my life" (paraphrased). He said it over and over through his writings. This is what this passage is leading to. We have to be the men and women God has called us to be if we're going to be effective in reaching the communities in which we live. That's the bottom line. It's our lives that say we belong to God. If they're not where they should be, then we send the message that you don't have to belong to God to be a part of this.

Disciple-making and church planting don't begin with a strategy; they begin with me. Am I the person God called me to be? If I'm not, what do I have to change to become that person? Until I change and become someone who loves God with all my heart, all my soul, all my strength, why would I expect God to use me?

All means all, and that's all it means. What have we kept out of our relationships with God? What have we stopped doing that God told us to do when we first became believers? We tell our teams all the time that if you're too busy to pray, you're too busy. Start cutting things out of your life. If you're too busy to spend an hour or two praying, you're too busy! If you're too busy to help someone, you're too busy. If you're too busy to make a difference at home and in your community, you're too busy. We spend our time doing the things that make us feel important rather than being the people God needs us to be in order to touch lives around us. We've been guilty of this. We are still guilty sometimes of filling our time with busy stuff so we feel important, instead of being disciple-makers in the midst of a lost generation.

If you are going to make disciples, then you have to be an obedient disciple of Jesus—not because others think so, but because you love Jesus more than anything.

12

PRAYER

In a meeting of the top one hundred disciple-makers in our ministry, we looked for common elements among these high-producing leaders. Each of these disciple-makers, along with the teams they led, started more than twenty churches per year. One group started more than five hundred churches in the previous year. We found many common elements among the different groups, but the only element that was present in every team was a high commitment to prayer.

These leaders spent an average of three hours per day in personal prayer. They spent another three hours in prayer with their teams every day. These leaders were not all full-time religious leaders. In fact, most of them had regular jobs. They started their days at 4:00 a.m., and by 10:00 a.m. were at work.

These top performers also spent one day per week in fasting and prayer. The whole team spent one weekend per month in fasting and prayer.

As we started looking at Disciple-Making Movements worldwide, we made a critical observation: a prayer movement precedes every Disciple-Making Movement.

There are two sides to catalyzing a prayer movement. First, we must become people of prayer. Second, we need to mobilize people to pray.

BECOMING A PERSON OF PRAYER

At the time of this writing, I (Paul) have been married for fifteen years. My wife, Christi, and I have three children, ages eleven, eight, and two. I run a recovery center for men overcoming alcoholism and drug addiction, a homeless shelter, and a food backpack program for displaced and homeless children, and I coach disciple-makers throughout the Pacific Northwest. I am an athlete, so I train a couple of hours each day. When we had our youngest child, Christi left a successful career as a public school teacher to become a stay-at-home mom. After we moved to the Pacific Northwest, we decided to homeschool our children. Christi bears the load of lesson planning for three different grade levels, on top of the responsibilities of running our home.

Our days, like a lot of people's, get pretty crazy.

Cultivating intimacy in the middle of all the craziness isn't easy. Life creeps in, and Christi and I communicate through lists rather than having conversations. Here is something I've learned: knowledge transfer isn't intimacy. It's part of intimacy, but if all communication comes in the form of texts and lists, intimacy soon disappears.

We've been trained to talk with God by reading Him our lists rather than having conversation. We mutter hasty sentence prayers as we race through our day without stopping and listening to what God has to say. We can't cultivate intimacy with humans like that, so what makes us think we can cultivate intimacy with God, who made us after His image, that way?

Maybe you've spent a lot of time talking *to* God but have little experience talking *with* God. Initially, the conversation may be awkward, but it will get better with practice. Intimacy comes when we set aside time to be together and are deliberate in how we use the time.

Say It Anyway

I love the sci-fi action flick *Serenity*. (I only recommend this movie if you like sci-fi action flicks. If you don't, you won't like it at all.) Malcom Reynolds (played by Nathan Fillion) is the sarcastic captain of an antiquated spaceship called *Serenity*. One of his crew, River Tam (played by Summer Glau), is a telepath. The bad guys who had previously kidnapped River tried turning her into a superweapon and caused her to go a little crazy. Malcom and the rest of the crew help her overcome incredible obstacles along her path to recovery. At the end of the movie, Malcom and River share a moment.

> **MALCOM:** So, you gonna ride shotgun with me, help me fly?
>
> **RIVER:** That's the plan.
>
> **MALCOM:** Think you can work out . . . [River launches *Serenity*, accelerating rapidly] . . . Okay . . . clearly some aptitude for . . . uh . . . It ain't all buttons and charts, little albatross. Know what the first rule of flying is? Well, I suppose you do since you already know what I'm 'bout to say.
>
> **RIVER:** I do. But I like to hear you say it.[1]

The moment I watched this scene, God told me, *Exactly. That's exactly how I feel.* I realized that, although God knows everything I'm going to say before I say it, He still likes to hear me say it anyway. He wants to hear me talk with Him. His omnipotence should never excuse a lack of conversation on my part.

Ask God for His Opinion

Have you ever walked out after a great movie and, rather than call or text your friends, talked with God about it? I talked with God about *Act of Valor*, a movie featuring active-duty Navy SEALs. In the first main action sequence in the movie, the SEALs have to rescue a female American intelligence operative from the hands of a terrorist. They bust in, kill the bad guys, rescue the badly beaten woman, and make a quick exit. Terrorists cut off several avenues of escape, and the SEALs finally have to ditch their vehicle in the river. Just as things look hopeless, two special warfare combatant-craft crewmen (SWCC) teams in their boats round the bend of the river and unload massive guns into the enemy vehicles, covering the SEALs as the SWCC teams pull them from the water. I love this scene. I've probably seen it more than a hundred times.

One time I decided to tell God about the scene. After I got done, I asked, "What is Your favorite part of the movie?" To my surprise and delight, He answered, *You know the part in the same scene where the SEALs go into the room where the woman is being held captive, tied to a wire bed frame? I like it when the SEAL cuts the ties holding her down and covers her nakedness with a nearby curtain. I like it when he says, "We are here to take you home." I like it when he picks her up and runs out to the waiting truck to whisk her to safety. I like it when he covers her body with his, protecting her from enemy fire. And I like it when, after the SEALs are pulled from the water, they take the time to treat her wounds. I like all of this because this is what I do.*

God rescues us from the evil one. He cuts the ties that bind us. He covers our nakedness. He protects us from the attacks of the enemy with His own body. And the Creator of the universe, Captain of angel armies, gently dresses our wounds.

Next time you get the chance, talk with God about your favorite movie. Tell Him what you like and don't like. Ask Him what He liked and didn't like. You'll probably never be able to view the movie the same way again.

And more important, the conversation will cultivate intimacy with God.

Become a Person Who Prays for Others

After our survey of the top disciple-makers on our team, I (David) changed my approach to prayer. Instead of recruiting people to pray for me, I would pray for them.

I took a piece of paper and numbered it from 1 to 30. Beside each number I wrote the name of a Christian friend. Next, I looked at my calendar. It was the twelfth of the month, so I called number twelve on my list.

When I called, I said something like this: "Hi, Landis! You are on my prayer calendar today. That means I'm going to be praying for you throughout the day. Is there anything specific you'd like for me to talk with God about on your behalf today?"

In this case, I was the first person to pray for him like this. Shocked, he thanked me and told me something on his heart that day. Then I asked, "Do you have time to pray right now?" He did, so I prayed with him. When we finished, he thanked me again, and we ended our conversation.

The whole exchange took five to ten minutes.

The next day, the thirteenth, I called number thirteen on my list and so on. By the end of the month, I spent a total of 150 to 300 minutes praying with others. I listened to the needs of thirty people. I prayed for thirty people. I encouraged thirty people. We developed deeper relationships because we prayed together.

When I can't call people, I text them. If e-mail works better, I e-mail them. When I e-mail or text, I write out my prayers. Writing my prayers keeps me accountable to actually pray for them, and when they read my prayer, they know they were prayed for.

If you want to be a disciple-maker, develop a life of prayer. Commit to pray for a different person each day of the month. Encourage them to find thirty people to pray for themselves, and so on. Before long you will see the hand of God move at the urging of His children as they pray in obedience to His will.

Listen to God

Prayer isn't about twisting God's arm to get Him to do what you think He should. It's about aligning your heart and mind with God's. Prayer is about spending enough time with God that you see His vision for His city (because it is His city) and His people (and they are all His people, not just the Christians). And as you spend time with God, walking the streets of His city, He whispers your role in His plan for the city. Not all at once, because that would be overwhelming, but little by little.

When I (Paul) arrived in Portland, I didn't have a clue where I needed to begin. Portland was a new culture with hundreds of new communities. I also had a new job. The levels of complexity were pretty daunting.

What do you do when you don't know where to begin? You pray. And I prayed a ton those first few months. As I prayed, I walked through the neighborhoods near my Rescue Center.

On one of my many prayer walks, I passed by a local strip club.

"Lord, please close that strip club. I don't want it to close because of a bad economy or because of some disaster. I want it to close because the men and women working there came to know you. I want it to become a facility used to reach the community, perhaps a church building. Show me how to reach the men and women who work there. I can't go in . . . I know my temptations and my limits. Show me how to reach them without exposing myself to that kind of temptation."

You know, I felt God respond, *the ladies who work here live in the neighborhood.*

"Really?"

When they get off work, they feel tired. They want to get home as quickly as possible so they can be safe and get some sleep.

"Okay."

And they do business in the area. You see that coffee shop?

"Yeah."

They drink coffee there. The nail place next door, they get their nails done there. The martial arts place up the road, the bouncers work out there. If you want to reach this community, find a couple of people—either a married couple or two young ladies—who would move into the neighborhood, get jobs, and hang out at those places. They will meet the ladies who work in that club.

Another time I was walking through a different neighborhood. This one felt closed. I got a sense that meeting people who worked here would be difficult.

"God, how do I connect with the people in this neighborhood?"

Once again, He answered me. *You see that kennel and dog-washing business?*

"Yeah."

Find a couple of people who would move into the neighborhood and start a dog-walking/pet-sitting business. They would get to know most of the people here, have keys to their houses, and get invited into their homes. That's one way to reach this community.

Luke 10:2 says, "And he [Jesus] said to them [the seventy-two], 'The harvest is plentiful, but the laborers are few. Therefore pray earnestly to the Lord of the harvest to send out laborers into his harvest'" (ESV). When I walked through the neighborhoods, God showed me ways to engage them (more on engagement later) and to allow Christians to engage lost people in casual conversations that lead to meaningful conversations, which lead to spiritual conversations, which lead to invitations to Discovery Groups (more on Discovery Groups later). Unfortunately, at the time of this writing, I still haven't found people willing to take this approach to reaching those communities. Women are still working at the strip club, and people are still walking their own dogs. I am still praying for, and actively trying to recruit, workers for these harvests.

Praying for God's Kingdom to Come and His Will to Be Done

Jesus prayed, "Your kingdom come, your will be done, on earth as it is in heaven" (Matt. 6:10 ESV). Using the parables of the Kingdom of heaven as prayer guides is an effective way to pray for your neighborhood. Take Matthew 13:1–9 (ESV), the Parable of the Sower, for example:

"A sower went out to sow . . ." *"Father, we ask You to send sowers out into this community to spread the news of the Kingdom of heaven among the people. May these sowers be godly men and women who love You. Raise them up to be leaders and servants. Guard them from temptation, and protect them from the evil one. Provide for their physical needs so they may focus on spreading the good news of the Kingdom and caring for Your lost sheep."*

" . . . some seeds fell along the path, and the birds came and devoured them." *"Father, we know that the good news of the Kingdom is often hard to understand. Sometimes it may even sound* harsh and difficult when it is full of love and joy. Please work to soften the hearts of people represented by the path. Open up their hearts and minds so they can hear Your Word, understand it, and receive it joyfully. We pray against the evil one, who wants to snatch the Word from their hearts before they even have a chance to think about it. Bind the evil one, and keep him from interfering as Your children have a chance to hear Your Word for the first time."

"Other seeds fell on rocky ground, where they did not have much soil, and immediately they sprang up, since they had no depth of soil, but when the sun rose they were scorched. And since they had no root, they withered away." *"Father, we are so excited when people receive the news of the Kingdom with incredible joy! Sometimes, though, we worry about the depth of their conviction. We know that when things get difficult, the people of the shallow soil may fall away because there was no depth to their faith. Please enable us as seed sowers to help build depth in all who hear Your Word and receive it with joy. May their roots of faith grow deep so they can withstand all persecution and temptations that would threaten their relationship with You."*

"Other seeds fell among thorns, and the thorns grew up and choked them." *"Father, life is difficult. So many things pull our attention away from loving You and living as Your children. Shield us from distraction. Protect us from losing our joy because life gets hard. Keep us from being unfruitful because our lives have become so full. We ask this for those who will hear Your Word as well— guard them from unfruitful lives. The evil one would keep them from bearing fruit that brings You glory and saves the lives of those they love. Protect them from his lies!"*

"Other seeds fell on good soil and produced grain, some a hundredfold, some sixty, some thirty." *"Father! We long to see the fruit that comes from the good soil! We want all who hear the good news of the Kingdom to bear incredible fruit! We want to experience their joy. We want to celebrate with them! We want to see You glo-rified and to worship alongside all those who come from second-, third-, and fourth-generation fruit. May we experience this fruitful-ness and this harvest in our lifetime. Amen!"*

Here is a list of the Kingdom parables in Matthew (ESV):

Parable of the Sower (13:1–23)

Parable of the Weeds (13:24–30)

[Parable of the] Mustard Seed and the Leaven (13:31–33)

Parable of the Hidden Treasure (13:44)

Parable of the Pearl of Great Value (13:45–46)

Parable of the Net (13:47–50)

[Parable of the] New and Old Treasures (13:51–52)

Parable of the Unforgiving Servant (18:21–35)

[Parable of the] Laborers in the Vineyard (20:1–16)

Parable of the Two Sons (21:28–32)

Parable of the Tenants (21:33–46)

Parable of the Wedding Feast (22:1–14)

Parable of the Ten Virgins (25:1–13)

Parable of the Talents (25:14–30)

Use these passages to guide your prayers for your commu-nity. Later, we will discuss using these passages as outlines for small prayer gatherings.

Listen to Lost People

"You're broadcasting when you should be tuning in." I think this is one of my father-in-law's favorite sayings. He's right; when I'm passionate about something, I dominate the conversation and stop listening to everyone in the room. I'm a lot better than I used to be, but I still have a long way to go.

When it comes to engaging lost people, many followers of Christ broadcast and completely forget about tuning in. Consequently, they become one more broadcaster in a very noisy world. When Christians don't tune in, lost people often tune them out.

Disciple-makers must tune in to their communities. They need to listen to what is going on and discern the felt needs of the community. Not only will this help them engage the community more effectively (more on that later); listening to the community will help them pray more effectively.

There is no substitute for being present in the community you want to reach. Walk the streets. Eat at the local restaurants. Drink at the local coffee shops and, if it doesn't violate how God has convicted you, perhaps the local pub or bar.

Watch the people. How old are they? Do they have children? If so, how old are their children? How do fathers and mothers interact with each other? How do they interact with their children? How do the people dress? Where do they typically shop? Are there bars on the windows of local businesses? Do the local businesses post Restrooms Are for Customers Only signs? Do people greet strangers? Do they make eye contact? Is there racial diversity? How do people of different races typically interact?

You may think you know what the community needs. But until you actually listen to the community talk—in their words—you have no idea how to pray. Go to school board meetings and town hall meetings. Schedule a ride-along with the local police department. Subscribe to local newspapers. Search online for local bloggers, Yelpers, tweeters, and Facebook groups.

Pay attention to what they say are the needs in their community. Listen to their perspective on local issues.

Ask questions. Remember, "Why?" questions can be confrontational. Use "Help me understand" statements instead. This isn't the time to confront, preach, or teach. *Understanding* doesn't mean "agreement." Understanding will give you a lot to discuss with God as you pray for your community.

God gave us two ears and one mouth for a reason. Perhaps He wants us to tune in more than we broadcast.

MOBILIZE PEOPLE TO PRAY

When the movement among the Bhojpuri began to gather momentum, the prayer network contained more than a hundred thousand people—before the Internet and e-mail really took off! Cityteam's Contagious Disciple-Making work in San Francisco and Latin America really took off after their team committed to prayer and fasting, as well as having more than fifteen hundred people committed to spend at least an hour a week—approximately ten minutes a day—in prayer, specifically praying for Disciple-Making Movements. Now there are 1,695 Discovery Groups in California and Central and South America, down to at least eight generations. Prayer is critical, and we cannot emphasize enough—you cannot have a Disciple-Making Movement without a prayer movement.

David and I hear missionaries in the United States and around the world complain, "I've been doing the stuff you said in your training, and nothing is happening. Disciple-Making Movement stuff just won't work here." We sympathize and ask some questions. In many cases, the missionaries worked very hard. They often have a pretty good personal prayer life. When we dig a little deeper, however, we find their prayer network is pretty small—usually a hundred people or less. We also discover their communication with their network consists of a monthly newsletter and the occasional emergency prayer request e-mail. While this may sound good, this level of communication with a prayer network this small is not likely to support any Disciple-Making Movements.

If you are a disciple-maker, you need to recruit, train, and mobilize an extensive prayer network—whether you earn your living as a disciple-maker or earn it another way. If you do not have a well-developed prayer network, you will be frustrated and disappointed as a disciple-maker.

Teaching People to Pray

People don't know how to pray for you. They don't know how to pray for your community either. If you want them to pray, you have to teach them.

We learn a lot by how Jesus taught His disciples to pray:

Now Jesus was praying in a certain place, and when he finished, one of his disciples said to him, "Lord, teach us to pray, as John taught his disciples." And he said to them, "When you pray, say:

"Father, hallowed be your name.
Your kingdom come.
Give us each day our daily bread,
and forgive us our sins,
for we ourselves forgive everyone who is indebted to us.
And lead us not into temptation."

And he said to them, "Which of you who has a friend will go to him at midnight and say to him, 'Friend, lend me three loaves, for a friend of mine has arrived on a journey, and I have nothing to set before him'; and he will answer from within, 'Do not bother me; the door is now shut, and my children are with me in bed. I cannot get up and give you anything'? I tell you, though he will not get up and give him anything because he is his friend, yet because of his impudence he will rise and give him whatever he needs. And I tell you, ask, and it will be given to you; seek, and you will find; knock, and it will be opened to you. For everyone who asks receives, and the one who seeks finds, and to the one who knocks it will be opened. What father among you, if his son asks for a fish, will instead of a fish give him a serpent; or if he asks for an egg, will give him a scorpion? If you then, who are evil, know how to give good gifts to your children, how much more will the heavenly Father give the Holy Spirit to those who ask him!" (Luke 11:1–12 ESV)

First, Jesus prayed. Teaching people to pray begins with your example. Cultivate a healthy prayer life. Learn to talk with God as you would a friend, as if He is sitting in the room with you (He is!). Walk your streets and talk with God about your community. As you do all of these, take someone with you.

Second, Jesus gave the disciples an example. Later on we'll talk about facilitating a prayer gathering. In these gatherings, you will help people learn how to pray through the Kingdom parables for their community. We will also talk about prayer walking and taking people along with you as you walk the streets in the neighborhood.

Third, Jesus talked about the disciples' attitude toward God as they prayed. We've already talked a lot about our attitude toward God and how it affects our prayers. Even as we transform our own attitudes about prayer and God, we have to bring others with us on that prayer journey.

Get Together to Pray

Facilitating a prayer gathering isn't difficult. If you've never done it before, it can be a little intimidating. Hopefully the following tips and outline will be helpful.

Invite a few friends and maybe some people you know from church over to your house to pray for your community. Let them know what time the meeting will start and end, and inform them that the majority of the time will be spent praying.

Plan to spend the first thirty minutes of the meeting getting settled, grabbing a cup of coffee, and maybe munching on some cookies. People need some time to be relational. Plan on it, but keep it to thirty minutes, or the mixing and mingling will dominate the time.

After the thirty minutes of mixing and mingling are up, gather people into a room to pray. Explain that you will use Scripture to help guide the prayer time, that you will read a verse or two and ask them to use that verse to inspire their prayers for the people in your community. Let them know you will pause after every few verses to allow them to pray out loud, as the Lord leads.

Here is an example of using the Parable of the Prodigal Son (Luke 15:11–45 ESV) as a prayer guide:

> **Read:** "And he [Jesus] said, 'There was a man who had two sons. And the younger of them said to his father, "Father, give me the share of property that is coming to me." And he divided his property between them. Not many days later, the younger son gathered all he had and took a journey into a far country, and there he squandered his property in reckless living.'"
>
> **Say:** *"Father, there are many in this community who take all that You've given them and squander it on things*

that will destroy them. Prostitution, alcoholism, drug abuse, materialism, and self-interest consume people in our community. Please protect them from themselves. Help us know what we need to do to serve our people in the middle of all this. Fill our hearts with compassion. These are spiritual problems that need You, Father, to answer them."

Allow people to pray as they are led.

Read: "'And when he had spent everything, a severe famine arose in that country, and he began to be in need. So he went and hired himself out to one of the citizens of that country, who sent him into his fields to feed pigs. And he was longing to be fed with the pods that the pigs ate, and no one gave him anything.'"

Say: *"Hunger is an issue in our community, as is self-ishness. Spiritual hunger is as real as physical hunger. Help us recognize those in spiritual hunger. Help us move past feeling helpless to make a difference in the lives of the spiritually hungry."*

Allow people to pray as they are led.

Read: "'But when he came to himself, he said, "How many of my father's hired servants have more than enough bread, but I perish here with hunger!"'"

Say: *"Oh Father! We long for the time when people will realize that You are the answer to their spiritual hunger! We long for the moment they recognize they are perishing. Please open up the eyes of those in our community to their spiritual reality."*

Allow people to pray as they are led.

Read: "'"I will arise and go to my father, and I will say to him, 'Father, I have sinned against heaven and before you. I am no longer worthy to be called your son. Treat me as one of your hired servants.'" And he arose and came to his father. But while he was still a long way off, his father saw him and felt compassion, and ran and embraced him and kissed him.'"

Say: *"Father, please move in the hearts of people in our community. Help us . . . help them . . . to become aware of our spiritual condition and our need for Jesus. Help us take the often-scary first steps toward You. Father, allow us to feel Your embrace as we turn to You. Allow us to be witnesses as people in this community turn to You and feel Your embrace."*

Allow people to pray as they are led.

Read: "'And the son said to him, "Father, I have sinned against heaven and before you. I am no longer worthy to be called your son." But the father said to his servants, "Bring quickly the best robe, and put it on him, and put a ring on his hand, and shoes on his feet. And bring the fattened calf and kill it, and let us eat and celebrate. For this my son was dead, and is alive again; he was lost, and is found." And they began to celebrate.'"

Say: *"Father, we can't wait to be able to celebrate the fruit of Your work in this community. Thank You for allowing us to participate in Your work. Allow us to celebrate with You and our new brothers and sisters! We thank You for that day and pray it comes soon!"*

Allow people to pray as they are led.

When you finish praying through the passage, or after an hour has passed, bring the prayer time to a close. Spend the last thirty minutes talking about what God said to people in the group as they prayed. Don't forget that prayer is about getting to know God's will for the community. This part of the prayer time is perhaps the most important.

Time is important in Western cultures. If you facilitate a prayer gathering in a Western culture, you need to know that. If you go beyond the time people allot for the gathering, they will be less likely to return. Also, the longer the event lasts, the less reproducible it is. Many people won't want to host—or attend—long events. For those who may have hired a babysitter, an event that goes too long will cause problems. Be considerate of cultural constraints, and don't push them if you don't have to.

Host prayer gatherings like this once a month. Encourage prayer partners to host their own gatherings. The goal is not to have one huge gathering. Instead, make it a goal to catalyze a hundred or so gatherings like this every month. These types of gatherings can be an effective way to mobilize anywhere from five hundred to a thousand people locally to pray for the community.

Prayer Gatherings for Nonlocal Prayer Partners

You need to recruit people to pray for you, your team, and your neighborhood who do not live and work in the area. Talk with relatives and friends, and see if you can speak to their church or their small group about what you are doing. Find people who are passionate about your mission, and ask them to coordinate small monthly prayer gatherings using the outline I just presented. Use Skype or FaceTime to join them at the beginning of their prayer meeting. Share—in one or two sentences—the need for Disciple-Making Movements in your mission field. Briefly share one prayer request, specifically focusing on something you will do to engage your community in the next week. Thank them for taking the time to pray for you, end the call, and let them get to it. Make sure to e-mail them the next week to thank them and let them know how God answered their prayers.

Encourage Your Network to Develop Prayer Calendars

Encourage your prayer partners to develop prayer calendars of their own. If you encourage ten friends to develop prayer calendars, your prayer network, including you, will pray for 11 people each day, or 330 people each month. As people pray for one another, a culture of prayer develops. As this culture emerges, God whispers His will to His people and guides them to join Him as He works to bring the people in the community to Him.

A culture of prayer creates an environment and spiritual posture God can use to mobilize His people to do His will and catalyze complete social and spiritual transformation in a community.

Take People on Prayer Walks with You

I became a huge fan of prayer walking after I read *Prayer-Walking: Praying On Site with Insight* by Steve Hawthorne back in 1996. I like the idea of prayer walking because when I walk and pray, I am less likely to fall asleep. Movement keeps me alert and focused much more than sitting or kneeling. Also, as I regularly walk through a neighborhood, God calls my attention to subtle changes in the community, opportunities for engagement, and potential partners. God wants the people in the community to know Him, so as I walk and pray, He brings my thoughts and ideas in alignment with His will.

Here are some tips we've gathered from miles of prayer walking over the years:

- Schedule the time. If you don't put a prayer walk on the schedule, you'll rarely take one.

- Plan the route. Prayer walks are easier if you know the route ahead of time.

- Dress appropriately. If the forecast calls for rain, dress for wet weather. If it's going to be cold, dress warmly. If it's going to be hot, dress to sweat. Nothing makes a prayer walk more miserable than getting caught with the wrong clothing.

- Plan for refreshments. Stopping at local stores and coffee shops would be ideal because you will get to interact with people in the neighborhood, but if it would be better for you, take a small backpack with a little water and some snacks. You don't want to be caught unprepared if you need a little pick-me-up.

- Don't stop walking to pray. Pray with your eyes open, as you walk. To outsiders, your prayer walk should look like two people talking as they walk through the neighborhood.

- Take a camera. If you have a camera in your cell phone, that will do. You may want to take a couple of pictures as you walk to include in your prayer updates. Your pictures may also help guide your prayers when you cannot walk the streets.

- Take a notebook. When God tells you something, stop at a bench or in a coffee shop and write it down. You don't want to forget it.

We recommend you take a personal prayer walk every other week. Take some friends along with you at least once a month. Encourage everyone on your team to arrange prayer walks personally, and with Christians in their networks.

Teach Your Prayer Partners to Pray with You Through the Steps of Catalyzing a Disciple-Making Movement

This book covers the first seven strategic elements necessary to be a Contagious Disciple-Maker and to catalyze a Disciple-Making Movement. Each strategic element has specific prayer points. You need to learn these points, not only to pray as you go, but also to teach others to pray for you and your team. Most people have no idea how to pray for you. If you want them to pray something more than, "Be with [fill in the blank] as she works with lost people in [fill in the blank]," then you need to teach them how to pray. Teaching them how to pray effectively is your responsibility.

Being a Disciple Who Makes Disciples

Being a disciple isn't easy. Sacrifice, spiritual warfare, and persecution all come with the territory. These can range from minor to more significant. Sometimes spiritual warfare and persecution can be life threatening. Choosing to be a disciple is a noble thing and, like most noble things, will require more than you know.

Find an inner core of people—maybe two to five—who know you and love you. Call or e-mail them weekly. Let them know what you're learning and what struggles you are facing. Get personal. If you can't trust them to keep confidences and shoot straight with you, they shouldn't be in this group. Have one or two very specific prayer requests to share every time you talk with someone from this group. Make sure to call, text, e-mail, or Facebook them and let them know how God answered their prayers.

Prayer

Having people pray about prayer sounds silly. But you have to develop a significant prayer network—one person or small group at a time—to pray for Disciple-Making Movements. Ask people in the network to pray for more people to pray. As they pray, family and friends will come to mind. They will ask them to join the prayer network. Just make sure you give them tools—online and offline—they can use to recruit others even as they pray.

Engagement

Engaging lost people requires creativity. Engagement activities can be as simple as paying attention to the people around you and talking with them. They can be as complex as organizing a summer sports camp or a humanitarian aid project. Either way, you will need plenty of creativity. Let people know what you want to do. Invite them to pray for creativity as you do it.

Ask your prayer network to pray for the right people to be engaged through the activity. The goal is not merely to serve people or to have fun—although serving people and having fun are awesome. The goal is to have casual conversations, which turn to meaningful conversations, which become spiritual conversations, which help you find the Person of Peace, and lead to an invitation to a Discovery Group. Educate your prayer network on this progression. Ask them to pray that you have the chance to talk with people. Ask them to pray specifically for each type of conversation. Don't take this lightly. If you do not engage people in these conversations and ultimately find Persons of Peace, your engagement activity failed. The chance for failure makes this an important prayer point.

Finding a Person of Peace

As you will learn, finding the Person of Peace is an act of God. He is the one who goes before and prepares a person, a family, an affinity group, and a community to bring the Gospel into their silo. We engage the community to find the Person of Peace and help him discover Jesus within a Discovery Group. The absence of a Person of Peace lets us know that we need to come up with a new way to engage other members of the community or move on. When you read through the chapter on the Person of Peace, make a list of all his characteristics. Have your prayer network pray for people to develop those characteristics within the community you want to engage.

Discovery Group

At some point, you will invite a potential Person of Peace into a Discovery Group. (You will learn more on Discovery Groups later.) You want her to accept and bring a couple of friends, or her family, with her in the process. Have your network pray for this. The group process is vital to multiplication.

As you read Scripture with the Person of Peace and her friends, have your network pray

- that they will engage with God's Word deeply

- that God's Word addresses questions they have about life

- that they will share what they read with friends and family who are not in the group

- that these friends and family will want to start Discovery Groups of their own

- that everyone in the group will change their lives as they read Scripture

- that their family and friends will notice the difference

- that they will listen to the Holy Spirit as God draws them to Him

You will face spiritual warfare throughout the process of being a Contagious Disciple-Maker. As the Person of Peace and her community read God's Word, they will experience spiritual warfare as well. Their lives will fall apart. Satan will do whatever he can to distract them and keep them from discovering Jesus. Since they don't know how to pray for themselves or how to weather spiritual warfare, you and your prayer network have to pray for them. Pray for their health, their relationships, their work, their rest. Pray for anything Satan might use to keep them from discovering Jesus.

Church

There is a major barrier between people discovering Jesus and deciding to commit their lives to Him. Demonstrating that commitment through baptism is an incredibly important moment. Pray the group will understand the importance of baptism. Pray they will commit to Christ and to one another. Read through the "One Another" passages in chapter 16, and pray that the emerging church develops these characteristics. Pray that they will reach out and serve the communities around them.

Leadership Development

There is a point where the disciple-maker moves on, leaving the emerging church to grow on their own. We will discuss this in depth later, but you can see how this is an incredibly important time for the church. Pray for emerging leaders. Pray for the Discovery Groups they've started. Pray for them as they mentor other leaders.

There are a lot of topics that will be covered as you read further in this book. Use the information you glean from those chapters to inform your prayers. Prayer throughout the process is incredibly important. Educate your prayer network. Make sure they understand that you cannot have a Disciple-Making Movement without a preceding prayer movement. Without prayer, everything will fall apart.

13

ENGAGE LOST PEOPLE

As more people gather in a space (like a city, university, or social club), like-minded people naturally form individual groups within that space. These groups eventually become large enough to be obvious to outsiders, people who do not belong to the tribe. These segments have distinctive boundaries, but are open to input and output. Social anthropologists call these segments "silos."

Most communities are a collection of smaller groups of people living and working in silos. University campuses also function this way.

How these silos gather and organize differs from space to space. Sometimes they gather along racial lines. In some places they gather along socioeconomic lines. They can also organize around affinity (although some affinities are more available to specific cultures or socioeconomic segments). Families are also micro-silos. Sometimes communities overlap. Often, people live, work, and play across multiple communities. There aren't any hard-and-fast rules about them; you have to spend lots of time researching and watching people within a space to see how they gather. Eventually, you see the patterns and identify the silos.

PERSONAL EVANGELISM, DISCIPLESHIP, AND SILOS

The most standard forms of evangelism have a common element—extraction. Extraction evangelism focuses on an outside leader (pastor, church planter, evangelist, missionary) who shares the Gospel with anyone who listens. In extraction evangelism, an individual is won to the Lord without serious regard for his or her silo. If someone using extraction evangelism techniques pays attention to silos, it is usually to figure out ways to access a group of people that hasn't yet been reached by the Gospel and to repackage the Gospel message (called *contextualization*) to make it easier to convert individuals in that silo. The individual conversion is more important than the possible disciple-making of an entire silo. Extraction evangelism is the result of poor theology and an evangelism strategy that does not understand silo structures, or chooses to ignore these structures.

Each person must make the decision to follow Christ for him or herself (Rom. 10:9–13). But, individuals coming to Christ outside the context of family or community are rare in Scripture and usually the result of unique circumstances, such as Saul, later known as Paul (Acts 9:1–19), and the Ethiopian eunuch (Acts 8:27–38). Jesus commanded us to "make disciples of all nations," not just individuals from all nations (Matt. 28:19–20). Mark and Luke say we are to preach to all creation and all nations (Mark 16:15–16; Luke 24:43–49). Acts 1:8 strongly suggests we should be witnesses to communities—Jerusalem, Judea, Samaria, and the ends of the earth. There seems to be a strong community/national emphasis in the Great Commission.

A common biblical statement regarding commitments to Christ is "so-and-so and his/her whole family/household believed and were baptized." This pattern emerges in Acts 10 with Cornelius. Peter defended his actions in Acts 11 (see also Acts 18:8; 1 Corinthians 1:16; 1 Corinthians 16:15). Individual encounters were expanded to the family quickly, and the family became the focus of the evangelism effort. At times this expanded to whole communities coming to Christ. (See John 4:1–26, the story of the woman at the well.) It was the Philippian jailer who experienced the miracle, but his whole family believed and were baptized (Acts 16:23–40). It was Lydia and a group of other ladies who first heard the message from Paul, but Lydia's whole household believed and were baptized (Acts 16:11–15).

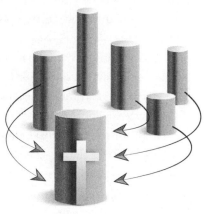

Traditional church planting pulls people out of their silos to create a new silo we call a church.

Extraction discipleship is similar to extraction evangelism. Unrelated people convert, are pulled out of their silos, and are brought together to form a new church. They learn a new culture, begin to speak an insider language, and are encouraged to bring others into the new community—if the outsiders are ready to leave their old silos. Redeeming their old silo is not a serious thought, though other individuals will be sought—if it is not too much trouble (in other words, little or no persecution). Soon, the new believers are so adapted to their new silo and so alienated from their old silo that it is next to impossible for them to reach their families, communities, or nations. Families perceive their loved ones as being stolen or kidnapped from them in much the same way Christians feel about cults and their practices. Silos are suspicious of anyone who would abandon his or her cultural roots. And nations rarely tolerate traitors.

Extraction churches find it very difficult to reproduce. The pain each member has experienced makes it difficult to inflict the same pain on others. Few members of extraction churches become effective disciple-makers, so the foreign or outside evangelist must continue to start each new church with the same disastrous results—individuals are extracted, families are fractured, communities are torn, and nations legislate against the evils of conversion.

In our opinion, Satan is at work in these extraction methodologies. Satan encourages the use of extraction evangelism and discipleship strategies because these strategies do not take silos into serious account, and the result is the "winning" of one at the loss of the rest of the family, community, or silo. These are good odds for Satan—he will encourage us to win one and lose ten or more as a result of these methodologies. Most of us play into Satan's hand, thinking we have done something great by "winning" one, when what we have really accomplished is the losing of a family, community, or silo as a result of extraction strategies.

Changing our evangelistic mind-set isn't easy. Extraction evangelism is ingrained in Western Christian culture. Yet extraction evangelism techniques create too many barriers to the Gospel to result in Disciple-Making Movements. Period. Extraction evangelism techniques even inoculate people against receiving the Gospel. Disciple-making, on the other hand, is part of catalyzing Disciple-Making Movements around the world. If Disciple-Making Movements are our goal, we have to make the jump from extraction-evangelism thinking to disciple-making thinking.

EXTRACTION-EVANGELISM THINKING	DISCIPLE-MAKING THINKING
Focuses on reaching one person at a time.	Focuses on reaching one family or community at a time.
Reaching one person is a success.	Reaching a family or community is a success.
Removes new believers from their existing community to become part of a new, branded Christian community.	Encourages discipleship with and within existing families and communities.
Transfers Christian culture to the new believer.	Redeems local culture.
Viewed by outsiders as destructive to community.	Viewed by outsiders as something new, but not destructive.
Results in increased levels of persecution in restricted-access countries.	Results in normal levels of persecution in restricted-access countries.
Painful for the new believer and his or her family—leaving one community for a new community.	Joyful process—the family discovers Christ together.

EXTRACTION-EVANGELISM THINKING	DISCIPLE-MAKING THINKING
Encourages believers to go back to their old communities to find people to bring to the new community.	Encourages believers to live like Christ within their existing community and share the Gospel as part of their daily life.

MAKING DISCIPLES, GOSPEL PLANTING, AND SILOS

What's the alternative? We must see individuals as doorways to families, families as gateways to silos, and silos as highways to nations. Our strategies must look past the individual to intentionally include his or her family, community, silo, and nation. We need to realize that the minimum unit for disciple-making should be the household (family), affinity group, or community rather than the individual, and that the group wins their community, the community wins the silo, and the silo wins the nation. When we focus on disciple-making rather than extraction evangelism, we find ourselves at odds with Satan instead of playing into his hand. And we develop strategies beyond simplistic personal extraction evangelism models that fail to keep pace with population growth, much less win nations.

The job of the disciple-maker is seeking the lost—all the lost. We must not stop when we have found one or a dozen or a thousand. We must not participate in strategies that cause lostness or promote lostness through neglect or misunderstanding the task. We must not contribute to strategies that intentionally fracture families or alienate communities from future encounters with Christ. Our job is to find the lost and save the lost, every last one. We may not be 100 percent successful, but we must not do anything that prevents the lost from receiving those who look for them, and being saved by the One who died for them.

We are in the business of redeeming communities for Christ and through Christ. We are not in the business of winning a few to a particular Christian culture, denomination, or church.

Contagious Disciple-Makers focus on planting the Gospel in each silo within a given space. Rather than specializing in personal evangelism techniques, a Contagious Disciple-Maker focuses on inviting and leading families or affinity groups within each silo in a Discovery Group that allows them to discover God as they read His Word. The Discovery Group encourages disciple-making, obedience, ministry, and leadership development. Consequently, Discovery Groups replicate within silos and jump the natural barriers between silos to replicate in other silos (remember, silos often overlap). The disciple-maker facilitates and guides the discovery process, models leadership, develops leaders, and encourages obedience, ministry, and disciple-making—without creating a "church" silo.

Gospel Planting focuses on planting the Gospel into every existing community rather than creating a new silo.

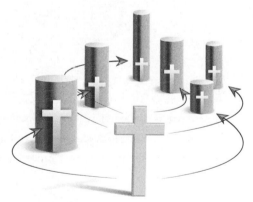

When groups come to the same realization Peter did—*"You are the Messiah, the Son of the living God"* (Matt. 16:16)—and are baptized, like Cornelius's household (Acts 10:47–48), they continue to meet as a family or affinity group within their silo.

Baptism signifies the reality that these groups within these silos are communities of believers, or churches. As they grow in knowledge and obedience to God's Word, these churches grow and replicate within their silos. In cases where they have relationships in other silos, they replicate across those relationships and start Discovery Groups in new silos. They don't bring friends from one silo into another for a "church experience."

Eventually the initial Discovery Group multiplies within the silo. Several groups will meet all within that silo.

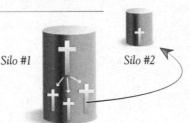

Silo #1   *Silo #2*

Because relationships span across silos, one group in silo #1 may start a group in silo #2.

BARRIERS

There are many barriers Disciple-makers have to overcome as they seek to engage silos, make disciples, and catalyze Disciple-Making Movements in communities.

A Personal Perception of Success

A lot of disciple-makers feel successful when they have a large crowd of people listening to their teaching and following their lead. Catalyzing Disciple-Making Movements, however, requires disciple-makers to give up the spotlight. Disciple-makers teach people to listen to God's Word and the Holy Spirit for answers, rather than being the person with all the answers. They develop leaders within the silo quickly and let them have the reins of leadership from the beginning. As nonmembers of the silo, disciple-makers must be satisfied with leading through leaders within the group rather than relating to each group personally, or even each person within the group.

Disciple-makers change their perception of success. They measure the number of leaders they train, the number of leaders those leaders identify and train, the number of tribes they engage, the number of groups they start, the number of groups that replicate, and the number of groups that come to Christ and are baptized.

Disciple-makers cannot base their success on the number of people in their group listening to their teaching (no matter how good it is) and expect to catalyze Disciple-Making Movements.

Expectations

Those who pray for the disciple-maker, support a disciple-maker financially, and partner with a disciple-maker, have expectations of what that person does and what makes him successful as a disciple-maker. If a disciple-maker partners with a local church, he will have to help them understand that his work will grow the church (we know this from experience with churches in similar contexts), but it won't look like it at first. Additionally, a disciple-maker may work a year or two before you see the exponential growth of a Disciple-Making Movement. Disciple-makers must think of ways to educate their partners about what they're doing and why.

Unrealistic expectations, or unaligned expectations, create major problems for disciple-makers if they want to catalyze Disciple-Making Movements. Educating people about vision for Disciple-Making Movements, and getting them to buy into the process, is a headache and may seem pointless. Developing relationships with people and partners who understand the vision and support the process, though, is vital for long-term ministry.

Identification

Some silos can be identified almost immediately, but pinpointing all the silos in an area and understanding each of their characteristics and boundaries takes time. Just remember, a disciple-maker doesn't have to have all the silos in an area mapped before she begins the process of making disciples within them. Silo mapping is something a disciple-maker does all the time as she ministers.

Firsts

Making disciples within a silo the first time may take a while. Figuring out how silos work takes time. Developing a team and training them how to engage silos also takes time. Don't get discouraged. Stick with the process and there will be fruit. (We know this from experience from working with silos and training teams around the world.)

SERVICE

Serving the community, or tribe, is the key to effective engagement and disciple-making. Jesus instructed His disciples to heal the sick, cast out demons, raise the dead, feed the hungry, take care of widows and orphans, visit the imprisoned, and preach that the Kingdom of God is near. Somehow, in the past hundred years or so, we have divided serving the community and making disciples into two separate camps. Disciple-making without service establishes a crippled church that will not obey Christ's commands. To serve the community and not make disciples puts a Band-Aid on a mortal wound. We may help someone find a new job or visit a sick person in the hospital, but he or she will still end up in hell for eternity if we or any other disciple never helped that individual discover Jesus.

Church is not church unless it serves the silo and makes disciples unapologetically. No apologies are needed when our actions match our words. We earn the right to share the Gospel based on how we serve. People notice how we serve, or don't serve, one another. It is obvious when we take care of our own but don't lift a finger to help someone outside our church. It is also obvious when we help those outside our church but don't make any efforts to meet the needs of our own church members.

I (David) have a friend who pastors a church in a small Texas community. He led his church to take up offerings for the fire department and the police department that helped them purchase much-needed equipment. His church has an incredible relationship with the rest of the community. With service like this, is it a wonder that this church is growing? When churches engage the community, assist those in need, and make disciples, they have high impact on lives.

In a recent meeting of African disciple-makers, one told the story of a disciple-maker providing the ladies of a village a donkey to haul water up from the river. No one had ever done this before, and it was a great help to the ladies, who had been putting water jars on their heads and walking up the steep hill to the village. The help led to questions of "Why?" The answers led to discussions about God, which led to a family coming to Christ and a church being started.

On one occasion, a friend commented that if we drive past a house in our community that has a broken window or a leaky roof and we do not fix it, we are not Christians. He went on to say that what transforms our communities for Christ is the meeting of individual and community needs. If we can do so personally, then we should. If the project is more than one person can do, then we should form ministry groups to meet the need. This shares the financial and/or time requirements to meet the need.

There was a lady in my community whose needs required more time than I could personally give. I recruited four other families to join me in the ministry to this lady. Together, we met her needs, and she became a believer. Her family soon followed.

I visited a country where Christian missionaries were forced to leave more than forty years ago and are still not allowed. When the missionaries left, a few struggling young leaders were in place. The government and the culture were highly anti-Christian. Many of these leaders gave up. But one young man committed himself to making a difference. In the forty-plus years since he was left on his own, he and his team have started more than three thousand churches, mostly underground.

In the beginning he tried to start churches the way his missionary mentors had trained him. But quick rejection by local leaders and opposition from the culture forced him to reconsider his approach. He looked at the needs of the people and began to meet the ones that he had the capacity to meet. At first, there were only a few things his knowledge and budget would permit him to do. But as he grew in knowledge, and as people came to the Lord through his efforts, his capacity increased. He began to meet greater needs, and more people came to the Lord. He built relationships through service that allowed him to share who he is spiritually, and others came to Christ.

Engagement starts with meeting the felt needs of the individual and tribe, which is the purpose of service. Engagement is not complete until those we have served have seen and heard the Gospel in such a way that they can say yes or no to the invitation to discover Jesus. If you want to reach the world for Christ, you must start with meeting the needs of those around you to the very best of your ability. If you want to reach the world for Christ, you must end with the Gospel; show those you serve that the Kingdom of God is near, and it can change their lives for all eternity. This is a huge part of making disciples.

Engagement is about entry into a tribe where we are strangers. Appropriate engagement is about entering this new community without adding additional barriers. In open countries, most disciple-makers enter a new community and announce they are religious workers, pastors, disciple-makers, or evangelists. In most, if not all, situations, this immediately adds tremendous barriers that limit or kill the opportunity to find the Person of Peace who will open the tribe to the gospel message.

The best engagement is through the introduction of a member of the tribe you want to reach. This can be a coworker, friend, family member, or almost anyone with whom you have a close relationship and who also has a good reputation within the community. A community member with a bad reputation is not going to assist in becoming an acceptable outsider in most communities. The higher the person's status, the likelier the community will accept the outsider.

When there is no one to introduce disciple-makers to the community, the disciple-makers themselves have to find acceptable ways to engage. These engagement methods are as numerous as one's imagination. We have had disciple-makers enter villages with a soccer ball and start a pickup game. Others have been itinerant salespeople of goods the area needs. Some have taken employment or worked on farms for their food. Meeting felt needs of education, medical care, safe water, and agricultural training have also been successful. Business that improves the local economy has been used successfully in many areas. The list is really almost limitless, and often these access opportunities require little or no financial investment.

Make sure to listen to the community before rushing out to plan new engagement activities. Engagement activities have to make sense culturally to the community you want to reach. The church is often guilty of creating awesome plans to engage lost people and putting a lot of resources into those plans without really stopping to think about whether their engagement activities make sense to the people they want to reach.

Think about it this way: Let's say you were driving through a community you wanted to engage and noticed a playground full of moms and children. You think, *Wow! This is a great place to initiate conversations, engage a community, and find Persons of Peace. How do I get them to talk with me, though?* After much deliberation, you might conclude that children like puppies and candy. Maybe you think, *If I take a puppy with me and give the kids candy, everyone will want to talk with me!*

Hopefully you see the problem. What would all those mothers do if a strange man showed up at the park, in the middle of the afternoon, with a puppy and candy? They would see you as a pervert and a threat to their children! If they didn't call the police, they would definitely leave. What began as a well-intentioned engagement activity would end up clearing out the park!

What if we shifted the plan a little? Let's say you take your wife, kids, and new puppy with you to the park. No one would think you were strange. Why? You have a culturally accepted reason for being at the park—your children. Culturally, you're safe—you have a wife and kids. Pretty soon, you will have a chance to meet and have casual conversations with most of the parents and children at the park. With time and consistent contact, some of those casual conversations may lead to meaningful conversations. Meaningful conversations turn into spiritual conversations. Spiritual conversations lead to an invitation for new acquaintances to discover God for themselves through the Bible. These conversations wouldn't be possible if, because of your actions, the community identified you as a threat before you ever had the chance to get to know each other.

USING BUSINESS TO ENGAGE COMMUNITIES

The disciple-maker walked up the path to the village. In all of his years of living and making disciples in the area, he never saw a walled village. Yet a huge wall surrounded his destination. Two guards stopped him at the gate.

"Can I come into the village?"

"No, strangers are not welcome in this village. We've had lots of problems with bandits. So we built this wall, and only people who live in this village can enter."

The disciple-maker realized he wasn't going to get into this village. So he moved on. A few days later, at a village about three walking hours away, he noticed a woman he had seen going into the walled village.

"Don't you live in that walled village?"

"Yes."

"What are you doing here?"

"This village has the largest market in the area. I come here to get things I cannot get in my own village."

The disciple-maker had an idea. "How often do you come to this village? What kind of things do you buy when you are here?"

The woman went on to tell him that she made the trip about once a week. In fact, most of the women in the village made the trip pretty regularly. She gave the disciple-maker a list of the things she bought on a typical visit. They chatted for a while and then parted ways.

The disciple-maker bought a bicycle and a cart. He purchased many of the products the woman in the market said she purchased regularly. After getting everything together, he rode his bicycle and cart to the walled village. "Is it okay if I set up my cart here outside the village?" he asked.

The guards looked at each other. After talking for a while, they came back to the disciple-maker and gave him permission to sell his goods on the road just outside the village gate.

As women left the village to make the long trip to the area market, they noticed the disciple-maker and his cart. When they discovered they could purchase everything they needed, the women were ecstatic. The enterprising disciple-maker and his cart saved them a six-hour journey.

The disciple-maker sold everything on his cart. He also made a fair profit, which the village women were glad to pay. He replenished his cart and made the trip to the walled village several times a week. He was well-known and liked by everyone in the village.

After a while, the disciple-maker started taking special orders. One day, an older woman ordered fifty kilos of rice for an upcoming wedding. The disciple-maker made a special trip to the area market and delivered the rice a couple of days later.

The older woman looked at the rice and then at the guards. "I cannot carry all this rice into the village. Can he just bring it in for me?"

The guards looked at each other. They liked the disciple-maker. Several times a week for several months, they saw him, talked with him, and watched him treat everyone fairly. "Sure."

The disciple-maker delivered the rice. From that day on, the disciple-maker delivered special orders inside the village.

Villagers invited him over for lunch. Soon, the disciple-maker found a Person of Peace, started a Discovery Group with his family, and planted a church in the village.

Business is a great tool for engaging communities and finding Persons of Peace. In fact, for-profit businesses and services are often more effective than not-for-profit organizations and services. People understand business but don't always understand nonprofits. Remember; engage silos in ways that make sense to them, not to you.

I (Paul) talked with a disciple-maker who found a new silo. He was excited because he realized the community didn't have a coffee shop. "I can start a coffee shop and use it to build relationships with people in the community! We can start a church out of the coffee shop!"

"Have you ever started a coffee shop before?" I asked.

"No."

"Do you have a friend who has started a coffee shop?"

"Yes."

"I tell you what," I suggested, "talk with your friend and see if he would do a feasibility study on starting a coffee shop in the area. If he thinks it would work, talk with him about partnering to launch the new shop. He could run the business; you can train the employees to engage customers and look for Persons of Peace. If he says it won't work, then don't do it. You'll spend way too much time and money in something that will ultimately fail as a business and fail as an engagement activity."

The disciple-maker talked with his friend. After doing some research, his friend said there was no way he'd be able to make a coffee shop in that community work. The church planter went on to look for a different way to engage that silo.

Keep in mind, if you want to use business to engage communities and silos, make sure it is a legitimate business, started to provide meaningful goods and services, and to make a profit. If you have problems making a profit, don't get into business. If you don't have business experience, partner with someone who does. The partnership will go a long way to making sure you do what God called you to do without getting swamped by all the demands of being a sole proprietor.

David and I get excited about engaging new communities. There is so much room for learning new things and applying them in incredibly creative ways. Between the two of us, we've learned about pocket watches, flown model helicopters, hunted, fished, run in a Tough Mudder, participated in endurance challenges (like GORUCK), studied Tae Kwan Do and Krav Maga, blogged, vlogged, led disaster relief teams, started a LAN café, served donuts and coffee to homeless men and women on the streets, and even become EMT certified. All of these activities allowed us to engage lost people who would never come to the churches we attend. All of these allowed us to have casual conversations that led to meaningful conversations that led to spiritual conversations. Sometimes we found Persons of Peace, and sometimes we did not. Regardless, we knew we were right where God wanted us to be—engaging lost people and seeking to join Him as He draws them home to Him.

14

FINDING A PERSON OF PEACE

An old man sat on the edge of the road approaching the village. When he saw me (David), he started. He slowly stood up and came to meet me.

"Finally!" he exclaimed. "You are finally here." Before I could say anything he took my arm and pulled me into the village.

"Here is the man I told you about," he told people as he pulled me along. "Here is the man I dreamed about every night for the last twenty years. My dreams told me that we must listen to everything this man tells us."

I shared the Gospel, and a church now meets in that village. God is at work in people's hearts even before we walk into their lives. According to this man, God had told him twenty years earlier that I was coming to his village. Funny thing is, twenty years before that moment, I was studying to be an engineer. I had no desire and no call at that time to be a minister or a church planter.

Making disciples and planting churches is easier if you're working with God and the people He has prepared rather than trying to force the Gospel on people who aren't ready. Engage a community, and then find the Person of Peace. Actually, if we do things right, the Person of Peace finds us. Learning how to be found is key.

The Person of Peace is not simply a good person or hospitable person or friendly person. There are many people in every culture who are good, hospitable, or friendly, but are not Persons of Peace.

The Person of Peace is the one God has prepared to receive the Gospel into a community for the first time. There are two major categories of Persons of Peace—some are Persons of Peace by nature, and some become Persons of Peace as a result of God's direct intervention in their families or communities. There are numerous examples of both in the Bible. Cornelius and Lydia are representatives of the "Person of Peace by nature" category. The Philippian jailer and the Samaritan woman at the well are examples of those who became Persons of Peace through God's direct intervention.

In all these examples, however, the disciple-makers were conspicuously spiritual people who lived out their faith without apology. This is the secret to finding the Person of Peace. We must live out our faith as conspicuously as possible. This is not about being religious. It's about being spiritual.

God condemns being religious. Look at how Jesus related and spoke to the religious leaders of His day and how God spoke through His prophets in the Old Testament. Religion was not well thought of or supported by Scripture.

God has a tremendous amount to say to us about being spiritual—rightly relating to God and His creation through a personal relationship with Him. This is about faith and living it out in all circumstances, regardless of consequences. It is about loving God and loving people. It is about obedient thinking and living. This kind of life draws in people who are interested in spiritual matters and opens the door to communities for establishing obedient bodies of believers whose Head is the Lord Jesus

Christ. We have to unconditionally live out a spiritual life to make evangelism and disciple-making happen.

So, in reality, finding the Person of Peace is more about us and the way we live than it is about finding the Person of Peace. If we are the people we should be, those who want to discover Christ come to us. This is more than just living a good life. It's living an obedient life that demonstrates the love of God and shares God's Word in such a way that the lost become saved, the saved become obedient, and the obedient make more disciples for the Lord Jesus Christ, resulting in self-replicating disciples and churches of Jesus Christ.

Finding the Person of Peace radically increased the number of churches we planted. We saw disciple-making teams go from planting a few churches per year to planting dozens of churches every year, and in some cases, even hundreds of new churches every year.

The Person of Peace strategy was developed from a composite view of Jesus' teachings when He sent out His disciples in Matthew 10, Luke 9, and Luke 10. Following are the commands Jesus gave to His disciples as He sent them out.

MATTHEW 10

- "As you go, preach this message: 'The kingdom of heaven is near.'" (v. 7)

- "Heal the sick, raise the dead, cleanse those who have leprosy, drive out demons." (v. 8)

- "Freely you have received, freely give." (v. 8)

- "Do not take along any gold or silver or copper in your belts; take no bag for the journey, or extra tunic, or sandals or a staff; for the worker is worth his keep." (vv. 9–10)

- "Whatever town or village you enter, search for some worthy person there and stay at his house until you leave." (v. 11)

- "If anyone will not welcome you or listen to your words, shake the dust off your feet when you leave that home or town." (v. 14)

- "I am sending you out like sheep among wolves. Therefore be as shrewd as snakes and as innocent as doves." (v. 16)

LUKE 9
(ADDITIONAL COMMANDS NOT CONTAINED IN MATTHEW 10)

- "Whatever house you enter, stay there until you leave that town." (v. 4) (This is different from staying only in the house of a worthy person.)

LUKE 10
(ADDITIONAL COMMANDS NOT CONTAINED IN MATTHEW 10 OR LUKE 9)

- "Go out by two ahead of Me to every town and place I am about to go." (adapted from v. 1)

- "Ask the Lord of the harvest . . . to send out workers into this harvest field." (v. 2)

- "Go! I am sending you out like lambs among wolves." (v. 3)

- "Do not greet anyone on the road." (v. 3)

- "When you enter a house, first say, 'Peace to this house.' If a man of peace is there, your peace will rest on him; if not, it will return to you. Stay in that house, eating and drinking whatever they give you, for the worker deserves his wages. Do not move from house to house." (vv. 5–7)

- "Heal the sick who are there and tell them, 'The kingdom of God is near you.'" (v. 9)

The Person of Peace teaching is an entry strategy to new communities. In the Great Commission Jesus commanded us to "go." What do we do when we get to where we are going? We find the Person of Peace.

This is radically different from traditional disciple-making methods. In the Person of Peace strategy, the disciple-maker has one job—find the Person of Peace. This person may be from any walk of life, but he or she will welcome you, listen to your message, help you with your livelihood, and allow you to stay in his or her home and influence his or her family and the community for the sake of the Gospel.

The disciple-maker does not do any of the traditional things required by traditional disciple-making. He does not preach or teach. He does not hand out tracts or sell books or give away Bibles. He does not do mass rallies or healing services.

Finding the Person of Peace starts with obedience to Christ and looks for where Christ is about to visit. This is evidenced by the presence of the Person of Peace. If there is no Person of Peace, then you move on. The Person of Peace is found through prayer and service. In our experience, this service is sometimes miraculous, as Luke 10 describes. Often, though, service is as simple as feeding the hungry or helping someone fix a flat tire. In both cases, the disciple-maker freely gives of him- or herself. We are told to pray for harvesters. The Person of Peace will be this harvester. We equip this person to be the disciple-maker for his or her community. We are to be as wise as serpents. This means we are to anticipate Satan's attacks and avoid them. We are to be as innocent as doves, gentle, and a threat to no one. We are to work or do business for our food, for a worker is worthy of earned wages. This avoids awkward questions regarding how we support ourselves. It also puts us at work when the rest of the community is at work, allowing us to meet people and have a reason to be in the community. All the ministries that Jesus commands us to do are about meeting the real and felt needs of the community. As we do this we are building relationships that allow us to talk about the Kingdom of God/heaven. The person who is responsive to this message becomes the focus of our attention. This focus is on the household, and we do not move around once the Person of Peace is found. We then make disciples of this family, who then takes on the responsibility of reaching their community for Christ.

We train disciple-makers to enter new communities after extensive prayer. When disciple-makers enter the community, they look for ways to meet the felt needs of the community through service, education, or business. As they meet these needs, they are meeting people and sharing openly about the Kingdom of God. When the Person of Peace reveals him- or herself, the disciple-maker shifts the focus to the Family of Peace. The disciple-maker starts a Discovery Group to help the family discover on their own who God is and how they must relate to Him. The disciple-maker teaches them how to study the Word of God, but does not lead the Bible studies or do any of the preaching and teaching. The focus is on the family learning directly from God through His Word. The disciple-maker guides the direction of the study, but does not conduct the study, except to model the process a few times in the beginning.

When the family comes to Christ, the disciple-maker helps them to move from being a Bible study group to fulfilling all the requirements of church. A leader is identified and trained to lead the group and to establish more groups through the family's network of friends and family. Disciples make more disciples. Leaders equip more leaders. Groups establish more groups. Churches plant more churches.

INSIDE AND OUTSIDE LEADERS

In traditional disciple-making, the outsider who starts a small group and plants a church often becomes that church's pastor. As a result, the *outside leader* becomes the *inside leader*. This makes traditional disciple-making almost impossible to rapidly replicate, and there is no reason to reproduce leaders, since the outside leader stays in charge. For Disciple-Making Movements to happen, the outside leader stays outside and trains, coaches, and mentors the inside leader, who in turn does the same with his or her people.

Now, the role of the outside leader is critical. This individual initiates the disciple-making process. This begins with prayer, vision, and planning. When the outside leader engages a community, he or she develops local relationships for the purpose of friendship, ministry, and discovering the Person of Peace. The Person of Peace gives the outside leader access to a family, affinity group, or community within a silo. As relationships develop, the outside leader introduces spiritual discussion topics that eventually lead to starting a Discovery Group.

Within the first month of the Discovery Group, the natural spiritual leader of the group becomes obvious. The outside leader focuses his attention on this inside leader. As soon as the inside leader is identified, group facilitation shifts from the outside leader to the inside leader. The outside leader teaches, coaches, and mentors the inside leader over the next two years or so.

As the inside leader matures, the outside leader's visibility diminishes to the point of being unseen. The outside leader's role becomes primarily a mentoring role that has no direct leadership in the new potential church. Leadership is through influence. Influence comes through maintaining the relationship and engaging in dialogue about leadership and group issues. Part of this relationship is a mutual accountability, including the spiritual, family, friends, community, church, business, and personal dimensions of life.

The responsibility of the outside leader is summed up in the following mantra: Model, Equip, Watch, and Leave. Disciple-making begins with the life and character of the outside leader. In private and public, the outside leader must be able to say with confidence, "Watch me and do what I do." Then the outside leader equips the inside leader in every area of life. To "equip" means to help a person grow to capacity, not simply to learn job skills or knowledge. The source information for this equipping is Scripture only. As the inside leader learns, the outside leader coaches the inside leader to practice what has been learned. At this point the outside leader enters a "watch" role to ensure that what has been learned is accurately reproduced. Then he or she leaves. This is not a sudden departure, but a gradual withdrawal from the process as lessons are learned and replicated in others. In the early stages the interaction between inside and outside leaders is frequent. As the inside leader matures, the frequency decreases.

The outside/inside leader relationship goes through many stages—teacher/student/learner, trainer/trainee, coach/player, mentor/mentee, and friends for life. These stages are fluid, but somewhat in order based on the task, the event, and roles. Sometimes the inside leader takes on the role of teacher, knower, trainer, coach, and mentor in situations where the outside leader is learning about the local inside leader's culture, customs, family, work, and so forth. This is a true give-and-take relationship.

The outside leader measures success by how quickly and how often the inside leader passes on what is learned. The final measure of success is when the inside leader becomes an outside leader for others, helping them become inside leaders in their own situations.

BE OFFENDED, BUT CHOOSE TO LOVE

I (Paul) once found an interesting silo online. A woman in the silo followed me on Twitter because she liked the way I talked about my family. As I read her blog, I realized she was a witch and was part of a community of porn stars, strippers, and people with various levels of involvement in the occult. The woman used foul language throughout her blog. Everything was pretty offensive.

Some people say that those actively seeking to engage lost communities should "choose to not get offended." We understand the sentiment, but some things really are offensive. They offend God and they offend us. So, not getting offended is really not an option. So what do we do with our offense? How would Jesus want us to respond?

One day, as I was praying, God showed me something. Jesus tolerated being in the same room with people who were unholy by nature. He ate with them, talked with them, and worshiped alongside them.

If we really believe that Jesus and God are one and the same, then we have to believe Jesus feels the same way about sin that God does. And God's stance on the matter is pretty clear: He hates sin. He cannot tolerate its presence. Sin results in death, and sinful beings cannot look upon the face of God and live.

Jesus was the sum total of all that is holy and terribly magnificent. And yet He ate with whores and tax collectors (read: traitors). He sat at the table with Pharisees, religious hypocrites consumed with self-righteousness. He loved Judas, the man who betrayed Him. He restored Peter, the man who denied Him. He drank from the Samaritan woman's cup, which was forbidden for Jewish men at the time. He allowed Himself to be arrested, beaten, and crucified. And Jesus—100 percent God—did not destroy anyone with holy fire.

Although their presence offended Him, He chose to give up His right to be offended. Why? Love. Love caused Him to suspend His right to be offended so that sinners could experience Him.

Love is the reason He still suspends offense. He still wants us to experience Him.

If you choose to work with people who do not follow Christ, you will be offended. If you choose to walk among the lost, you will see, hear, and read things that make your blood boil. But you have to love people more than you are offended if you want them to have the slightest chance of experiencing Christ's love.

We offend Christ every time we choose our way instead of His. That is, we offend Him every day. God's love is the only thing that saves us from destruction.

So, we allow ourselves to be offended as well. We choose, however, to love people enough that our offense fades in comparison to the love we have for them and the desire we have to see them fall in love with Jesus.

FINDING A PERSON OF PEACE AT STEAK 'N SHAKE

A friend of mine walked to the cash register to pay for his meal. As the young Steak 'n Shake employee took the money, he asked my friend a question, "Do you think it's possible that if you prayed hard enough, your family would go to heaven?"

Taken aback, my friend paused. People in Ohio don't start conversations like this, certainly not with complete strangers. He realized the young man was a potential Person of Peace. In the two years since he received training about Contagious Disciple-Making, he worked hard to be a disciple who made disciples and to be a person of prayer.

"Do you have a Bible?" my friend replied.

The young man hesitated, then said, "Yeah . . . yeah . . . I do."

"When you get home, take it out and look up the book of Luke, chapter 18, verses 1–8. I'll come back in a couple of days, and you can tell me how God answered your question."

The young man agreed. My friend finished paying for his food, gathered his family, and went home.

A couple of days later, he went back to Steak 'n Shake. Sure enough, the young man was there. "Did you get a chance to look up that story?"

"I did!"

"What did God tell you?"

"It is possible to pray hard enough that your family would go to heaven." Then his face fell. "But, you will never know until you stand in front of the judge."

My friend leaned forward, "Would you be interested in knowing a way that you and your family can know for sure that you will enter the Kingdom of heaven? "

The young man lit up. "You can do that?"

"Yes, you can! I tell you what: when you go on break, come over to this table and I will show you what you need to do."

Later, the young man joined him at the table. My friend led him through a Discovery Study of Genesis 1:1—2:3. (We cover Discovery Groups and Studies in the next chapter.) He told the young man to go home, gather his family, and repeat the study with them, and that he would return to Steak 'n Shake next week to see how things went.

The next week, my friend returned. He waited for the young man to go on break and join him at the table. "How did it go?"

"Dude . . . that was the most incredible thing I have ever done with my family!" The young man leaned forward. "Do you think it would be okay to do one of these Discovery things with my friends, as well?"

My friend's experience illustrates several important lessons.

Becoming the kind of person who attracts a Person of Peace takes a while.

My friend attended Contagious Disciple-Making training two years before he encountered the young man at Steak 'n Shake. This wasn't a passive waiting time for him, though. He worked to become a conspicuously spiritual person. Already a pastor of a church, he applied the principles of Contagious Disciple-Making with his congregation. He gathered a few friends to pray regularly and developed a prayer calendar.

Finding a Person of Peace requires an act of God.

As my friend grew as both disciple and disciple-maker, God included him in His plans to reach out to lost people in his community. God worked, through the Holy Spirit, to prepare the young man to hear His Word. He moved to bring my friend into Steak 'n Shake at the right time. God prompted the young man to ask the question, and He prepared my friend to respond. God is the center of reaching the world. We have to listen and join Him in His work.

You need to qualify potential Persons of Peace.

Jim, a friend and longtime missionary, told me that Persons of Peace have three primary characteristics: They are open to a relationship with you. They hunger for spiritual answers for their deepest questions. And they will share whatever they learn with others. Jim likes to use the acronym *OHS* to remember these characteristics: Open, Hungry, Sharing.

The young man at Steak 'n Shake was obviously open. He approached my friend. His question, and the fact that he looked up and read the parable, indicated that he hungered for spiritual answers to his questions. Finally, he shared with his family, and the thought of sharing with his friends excited him.

Don't assume every friendly person is a Person of Peace. Instead, attempt to qualify them as my friend did with the young man at Steak 'n Shake.

Don't facilitate every group.

My friend facilitated the first meeting with the young man. The young man immediately went and replicated the meeting with his family. My friend never met the young man's family. But by asking lots of questions, he knew how the study went and what questions that family had. From the first meeting, my friend developed the young man as the leader of the group.

FINDING PERSONS OF PEACE AT A POKÉMON CLUB

So many thoughts whirled around in my head as I drove to my neighborhood Target store. *How can I connect with my kids better? What can I do to engage my community and find Persons of Peace? My kids are getting invited to sleepovers. How am I going to get to know their parents? My son has been pestering me to play* Pokémon. *I need to play with him tonight.*

Suddenly, all these thoughts came together in a single realization—I could start a Pokemon club! Starting one would make me an instant hero to my kids! Since many of their friends played the game, I would have the chance to meet them and their parents. Parents could come and talk with one another while their kids played the game. The conversations would give me a chance to look for Persons of Peace. A Pokémon club sounded like a very cool engagement activity.

But where would we meet? I didn't want to offer my house. My wife would kill me. I traveled quite a bit and didn't want to rope her into something she would have to keep going while I was out of the country.

When I pulled into Target, the final piece fell into place. This particular store had a large area with several tables. Families could buy Starbucks or Pizza Hut and sit down to eat. The area had about twenty tables, and they were rarely full. In fact, at 6:00 p.m. on a Saturday night, all the tables were empty. We could have our meeting there! As long as parents bought coffee or pizza, Target probably wouldn't have any problem with us using the space. To top it off, Target sold Pokémon cards! The kids could purchase and trade cards right there! Instant win!

I ran the idea past my wife when I got home. She thought it was a great idea. I told the kids, and they got really excited. We scheduled our first meeting the following weekend. I told the kids to invite their friends.

Our first meeting was a success. Several kids and their parents showed up. Everyone had a great time. I had some great conversations with parents. Connecting faces with the stories my kids told me after school was nice.

Over the next few weeks, the Pokémon club grew. Some older kids we knew from Tae Kwan Do joined us and played a different trading card game. They invited their friends, and the club grew. They even met when I was out of town!

One week I had a good conversation with one of the dads. His son was thirteen and had had a rough week. This dad shared his frustration with me.

"Parenting isn't easy these days," I replied. "I don't know how I'd do it if God didn't give me wisdom."

He paused for a minute, and then continued the conversation.

The Pokémon club created a great atmosphere that allowed me to have fun and to engage in casual conversations that had the potential to lead to meaningful conversations, which could lead to spiritual conversations, which then might give me the chance to identify Persons of Peace and invite them into a Discovery Study. I didn't hand out tracts or spiritual literature. I didn't wear T-shirts with a Christian message. Instead, I waited for appropriate opportunities to indicate that I was a spiritual person, in a safe place to have spiritual conversations. In the case of the dad and his teenage son, the casual conversation did lead to a meaningful conversation. When it felt appropriate, I interjected a statement that indicated that parenting is hard, but God gives me wisdom to parent well. The statement wasn't offensive.

In its context, it wasn't trite either. The dad heard it and decided to move on. As far as I could tell, he wasn't offended. The conversation continued quite naturally. Had the dad been a Person of Peace, he would have used the opportunity to make the conversation more spiritual. If he didn't do it at that time but was still a Person of Peace, he would have at another time. He didn't do either, so I knew he wasn't a Person of Peace and moved on.

I saw him several times after that. We had some good conversations, but they never drifted to spiritual topics. As I said, he wasn't a Person of Peace.

SHAKING THE DUST OFF YOUR FEET

Finding a Person of Peace is exciting and hard work. So many people we train get pumped when they talk about their ideas for finding Persons of Peace and starting Discovery Groups. Leaving when you don't find a Person of Peace is something no one wants to talk about. Yet, Luke 10:10–12 says, "But when you enter a town and are not welcomed, go into its streets and say, 'Even the dust of your town we wipe from our feet as a warning to you. Yet be sure of this: The kingdom of God has come near.' I tell you, it will be more bearable on that day for Sodom than for that town." Remember, Satan wants to suck up all our time engaging people who aren't ready, or who are unwilling, to discover Jesus. If we don't leave, we might not find the Person of Peace waiting in the next family, affinity group, community, and silo.

A disciple-making friend of mine told me about a young professional he trained. This young man had graduated from college, and he got a well-paying job. In his mind, the job would allow him to engage a new community and find Persons of Peace.

After working there for quite a while, the young professional decided there were no Persons of Peace to be found. So he got another, lower-paying job. As he packed his office, his coworkers approached him. They wanted to see what was wrong. They couldn't imagine leaving a job unless you completely hated it and hated your coworkers. The young professional reassured them that the job was great and they were great.

"Then why are you leaving?" they wanted to know.

"I got this job to search for people who had spiritual questions. I feel my purpose is to help people discover God for themselves."

"What do you mean?" they asked.

The young man went into more detail. Ultimately, several of his coworkers indicated that *they* wanted to discover God. The young professional went on to his new job but returned to his former job regularly to facilitate a new Discovery Group.

Disciple-makers join God where He is working. The presence of a Person of Peace lets the disciple-maker know God wants him or her to engage the community deeply, that the harvest is ready. We partner with God to bring in the harvest. If the harvest isn't ready, we don't need to bring it in early! Instead, we move on to another field, another community, and look for Persons of Peace there.

We may leave communities, but we don't forget them. We send prayer teams back into communities we leave. They prayer-walk the streets, asking God to work in the hearts of people in the community. They ask God to develop Persons of Peace. They ask for wisdom, that He will let them know when they are to return to the community. Six months to a year later, we send disciple-making teams into the area, engaging the people again, looking for a Person of Peace. In many cases, we find Persons of Peace the second time we engage a community, after extended prayer.

15

DISCOVERY GROUPS

The instructor put an image up on the screen. "I want you to take a look at this image," he said. After a few seconds, he blanked the screen. "Now, describe the image."

People called out various things they remembered. The instructor allowed them to continue just until they started repeating things that others had said already.

Finally, he put the picture back on the screen. "Could any one of you remember everything in this image?"

A collective "No" swept through the audience.

"Yet, together, you manage to remember most of the details in this painting. Now that you've heard everyone list what they remembered, I'll bet that you remember more of the image than you did before we talked about it."

The instructor looked around the room, then continued: "Group memory is better than individual memory. And as groups recall what they remember, their collective memory becomes the memory of the individual. This is one of the many reasons groups, and the group process, are essential to starting movements."

There are several reasons groups are so powerful:

Groups remember more than individuals. As demonstrated with the picture exercise, a group of people can remember more, and more accurately, than an individual. As groups recall things together, group memory becomes the memory of each individual in the group.

Groups learn faster than individuals. Groups require less repetition of facts and principles before they can recall them collectively. As we've said before, the group recollection process causes group memory to become individual memory. Consequently, the learning process is greatly accelerated in groups when you allow the group process to happen.

Groups replicate faster than individuals. Because groups remember more and learn faster, individuals within a group rapidly reach a point at which they can pass on what they know to others. Since each individual was discipled within the group process, they naturally use the same process to disciple new groups—within their own silo or in a neighboring silo.

Groups replicate more often than individuals. Since members of a properly led group get to a point of replication very quickly, they can replicate more often. They know how to plant what they know into groups within their silo, or in neighboring silos, so individual group members replicate themselves within other groups. This allows group members to replicate with more people than if they focused on individuals.

Groups are a protection against bad leadership and heresy. When the authority of Scripture and the Holy Spirit is part of group DNA and group process, groups can protect themselves against bad leadership. Groups that measure what leaders say against Scripture can easily stop the actions of leaders who try to implement extrabiblical, or even unbiblical, policies and procedures. Consequently, the effects of bad leadership are reduced, bad leaders are removed, and heresy is avoided.

Groups self-correct. This is the reason well-discipled groups protect against bad leadership and heresy. Group members understand the Scripture they read and correct one another when someone introduces an interpretation or application of Scripture that isn't apparent in the passage.

Groups keep individuals accountable. If you plant the Gospel in established silos and groups, group members see one another enough to hold each other accountable. If a group member disobeys Scripture, the group can become aware of his or her disobedience rather quickly. Properly discipled groups address this disobedience and help in the repentance and restoration of their disobedient member.

DISCIPLING GROUPS

When you engage existing groups within silos, you reduce many cultural barriers that slow down (or stop) group process. Families have existing authority structures. Well-established affinity groups already have leaders and followers. That said, groups still need to be discipled. In other words, they need to be taught how to study the Bible together, how to discover what God says through His Word, how to change their lives to obey God's Word, and how to share Bible passages with friends and family. Groups don't do these things naturally; they have to be discipled into them so that they become as natural as breathing.

Use Existing Groupings

We've already discussed, at length, the benefits of engaging existing groupings within their silos rather than starting groups that are a composite of people from different silos.

Establish DNA Early

Groups establish the habits and DNA for meetings very quickly—by the third or fourth meeting. Groups are very resistant to change once they've established their pattern for meeting. Consequently, group DNA must be established during your first meeting with the group.

Establish DNA Through Action

You cannot tell people what DNA they need to have. You have to get them to do things or think about things in a way that leads them to build habits. These habits become DNA. If you establish DNA well—through action, not instruction—groups will replicate that DNA naturally within their silos and in overlapping silos. We will talk about this more in the "Group Process" section.

Establish DNA Through Repetition

Group DNA is the product of what you do, and do often. You cannot do something once or twice and expect it to become DNA.

WHAT DNA DO YOU NEED FOR GROUPS THAT MULTIPLY?

A missionary attended a few of our trainings and worked hard to implement them in Honduras. After a year of trying, this missionary was about to declare that Disciple-making Movement methodologies wouldn't work there. After a week with his team—almost all Hondurans—we realized that the missionary had adapted the Discovery Group meeting. Consequently, groups they started were leaving out several elements of the study—important DNA elements for multiplication—and were not replicating the Discovery Group blueprint.

Several members of the missionary's team did not want to make the necessary changes. He lost all but six members of his team. We also told the missionary that his team members needed to work in pairs, instead of going to villages individually.

Instead of fourteen individuals traveling to fourteen places, this missionary now had only three teams of two. The missionary thought we were crazy, but he and his remaining team members were thoroughly committed to the process.

In the year after that trip, they started three hundred Discovery Groups. Many were third-generation groups—a group that had been started by a group that had been started by a group.

There is a minimum DNA required for groups to replicate past the first generation. Let's take a look at each element.

Prayer

Just as prayer is an essential element of movements, it is also a critical element of groups. From the first meeting, we embed prayer in the group process. Remember, we never ask lost people to bow their heads and pray. We don't explain what prayer is. We don't have a lecture about this being an important part of group DNA. Instead, we introduce a simple question, "What are you thankful for today?" Each person in the group shares. Later, after they choose to follow Christ, we say, "You remember how we open each meeting with the question, 'What are you thankful for?' Now, as followers of Christ, we talk with God the same way. Let's tell Him what we are thankful for."

Intercession

All intercession is prayer, but not all prayer is intercession. That is why we separate intercession and prayer. Intercession involves sharing personal concerns and stresses as well as the concerns and stresses of others. A simple question—"What things have stressed you out this week?"—introduces this DNA element to groups of lost people. Again, each person shares. After the group becomes a baptized group of believers, we say, "In the same way that you shared things that stressed you out with each other, now you can share those same things with God. Let's do that now."

Ministry

We define ministry as "God using His people to answer the prayers of the lost and of the saved." As any group—lost or saved—shares needs, there is going to be a group desire to make a difference. All the group needs is a little nudge. Ask the question, "As we shared things that stressed us out, is there any way we could help each other during the coming week?" Follow it up with, "Do you know anyone in your community that needs our help?" Embed this DNA from the beginning and you won't have to worry about motivating the group to transform their community when they become Christian.

Evangelism/Replication

Did you know that lost people can evangelize? Well, they can if you keep it simple enough. Evangelism, at its core, is sharing the Gospel with someone else. When working with lost people, they don't know the whole Gospel. That is totally okay. We just want them to share the story they just heard with someone who wasn't in the group. We get them to think this way with a simple question, "Who do you know that needs to hear this story this week?"

If that person is interested, rather than bringing her into the existing group, we have the first lost person start a group with her, her friends, and her family. So the first lost person experiences the study in his original group and then replicates the same study in the group he started with his friend.

A disciple-maker told the story of a young college student on his team. This student carried one of those small whiteboards in his backpack. Whenever he sat down in a common area to study, the young man took the board, prayed over it, wrote whatever he felt God tell him to write, and displayed the board next to his backpack as he studied.

On one particular day, the young man wrote something like, "You are not an accident." Several people approached him throughout his study time: "What do you mean, I'm 'not an accident'? I was an unplanned pregnancy." Or, "Thanks. I needed to hear that today." The young man listened to them and talked with a couple for a while. Eventually, he said something like, "You know, you have some pretty good questions. There are some stories in the Bible that answer those questions. Why don't we meet in your dorm tonight and read the stories together. And why don't you invite some friends that might have similar questions."

Later that evening, the young man facilitated a Discovery Group with the students and their friends. The next week, at their second meeting, one of the student's friends approached the young man and asked, "Do you think it would be okay if I invited one of my friends to this group? "

"I tell you what," the young man replied, "I will help you start a group like this with your friend and some of their friends."

The young man coached the student through starting a group of his own. Over the next few weeks, the young man coached three additional groups into existence—all of them started before any members of the first group were baptized!

We know this sounds crazy. Stick with us and some of the questions we know you have right now will be answered in a bit.

Obedience

As we said before, obedience is a critical element of Disciple-Making Movements. It has to be present even at the small group level, even with groups of lost people. Now, we don't look at groups of lost people, shake our fingers, and say, "You must obey this passage." Instead, we ask, "If you believed this passage is from God, what would you have to change in your life?" Remember, they may not even believe in God yet, so "If" is totally acceptable.

When they choose to follow Christ, you adjust the question, very slightly. "Since you believe this is from God, what are you going to change in your life?" Because they've been asked this question all along, new believers don't struggle with the idea that they need to obey God's Word, that it requires something of them, that it requires them to change.

Accountability

Building accountability into the group DNA starts in the second meeting. Look at the group and ask, "You guys said that you were going to help so-and-so this week. How did it go?" Also ask, "Several of you identified things that needed to change in your life. Did you make those changes? How did that go?" If they didn't do anything, encourage them to give it a try this time and be ready to share what happened the next time you get together. Emphasize that it is important for the group to celebrate everyone's accomplishments.

Initially, this will surprise everyone. They won't expect it. For the second meeting, however, several will be ready. After the third meeting, everyone will know what is coming and will be prepared.

Obviously, this practice continues after everyone is baptized.

Worship

You can't ask lost people to worship a God they don't believe in. You shouldn't force them to lie by singing songs they don't believe. Still, planting the seeds of worship into the group DNA is possible.

When they talk about things they are thankful for, it will become worship.

When they talk about the changes they made in their lives as they respond to Scripture, it will become worship.

When they celebrate the difference they made in their community, it will become worship.

Despite what is being communicated at many churches today, worship songs are not the heart of worship. Rather, worship is the product of a relationship with God. Singing praise songs is one expression of the joy our relationship with God brings.

Yes, eventually your group will sing praises. The DNA for worship, however, is embedded long before they start to sing.

Scripture

Scripture is central to the meeting. The group reads Scripture, discusses it, practices recalling it with each other, and is encouraged to obey it. Scripture does not take second chair to any teacher. Scripture *is* the teacher. We'll discuss this more in the next group DNA element.

Discovery

When working with lost people, we have to avoid falling into the role of explaining Scripture. If we do, we become the authority rather than allowing Scripture to be the authority. If we are the authority, replication is limited by our leadership capacity and the time we have to teach every group. Consequently, shifting from Scripture being the authority to the teacher being the authority will keep groups from replicating as they should.

This is a hard shift to make. We love teaching. It makes us feel good. We know the answers and want to share that knowledge with others. But if we want to disciple people who look to Scripture and the Holy Spirit for answers to their questions, we can't be the answer-people. We have to help them discover what God says to them in His Word.

To reinforce this idea, we call the outsiders who start groups *facilitators*. They facilitate discovery rather than teach. Their job is to ask questions that get lost people to examine Scripture. After they read a passage, they ask, "What does this passage say about God?" and "What does this passage tell us about humankind?" and "If you believed this was from God, what would you have to change about the way you live?"

The discovery process is essential to replication. If groups do not learn to go to Scripture and rely on the Holy Spirit to answer their questions, they will not grow as they should and will not replicate much, if at all.

Group Correction

A vast majority of our group leaders and church leaders have no institutional biblical training. When people hear this, they ask, "What about heresy? How do you keep your groups from going crazy?" This is a great question that, as leaders, we should ask.

First of all, all groups have the tendency to be heretical in the beginning. They don't know everything about God's Word. They are in a process of discovering God, which moves them from disobedience to obedience, but it is impossible for them to know everything from the beginning. As the group reads more together, as they discover more about how God wants them to relate to Him, they become less heretical. That is part of discipleship.

If we see them going too far away from Scripture, we'll immediately introduce a new passage and lead them through the Discovery Group process on that passage. (Notice that I didn't say, "teach" or "correct." The Holy Spirit will use Scripture to correct their behavior. They just need to be directed to the right passage.) After they go through the additional study, they recognize what they need to do. More important, they actually do it.

Second, we need to realize that heresy usually begins with a highly charismatic leader with some education (I'm referring to personal magnetism, not the religious movement!), who teaches the group what the Bible says and what they must do to obey it. In this case, groups accept what the leader says and never examine it in the context of Scripture.

We teach groups to read the passage and examine how each group member responds to it. Groups are taught to ask a simple question, "Where do you see that in this passage?" When someone makes a weird obedience statement, the group asks this question. When someone adds in a detail when she retells the passage, the group asks this question. This question forces all group members to focus on the passage at hand and explain their insights and obedience.

The facilitator models group correction. They also model focusing on the passage at hand.

Priesthood of the Believer

New believers and not-yet believers need to realize there are no intermediaries standing between them and Christ. We have to embed DNA that removes the barriers and perceived intermediaries. That is why Scripture must be central. It is also why outsiders facilitate rather than teach. And it is why the group is taught to self-correct based on what Scripture says.

Yes, leaders emerge. They have to. It is natural. But leadership is identified by functions that define a role. Leaders do not belong to a different class of spiritual or special status. If anything, leaders are held to a higher level of accountability, but their accountability doesn't give them special status.

If the DNA for the Priesthood of Believers is not present, you will never have a church. The discipleship process must establish this DNA.

WHAT DOES A MEETING LOOK LIKE?

That is a ton of explanation for something that is really quite simple but very deliberate. The question is, "What does it all look like when you fit it into a meeting?" Here is a simple outline with the DNA elements in parentheses:

- Ask: "What are you thankful for this week?" (Prayer/Worship)

- Ask: "What has stressed you out this week? What do you need for things to be better?" (Intercession)

- Ask: "What are the needs of the people in your community?" (Ministry)

- Ask: "How can we help each other with the needs we expressed?" (Ministry)

- Ask: "What did we talk about last week?" (Accountability)

- Ask: "Did you change anything in your life as a result of last week's story?" (Accountability/Obedience)

- Ask: "Did you get a chance to share the story with [the person they identified]?" (Accountability/Worship)

- Ask: "We identified several needs last week and planned to meet those needs. How did it go?" (Accountability/Worship)

- Say: "Let's see what the Bible teaches us this week. Read this week's passage." (Scripture)

- Ask for someone to retell the passage in his own words, as though he were telling a friend who wasn't there. (Accountability/Evangelism)

- Ask the Group: "Do you agree with that retelling? Is there something he added or left out that he shouldn't have?" As long as the group doesn't miss a key component of the passage, continue. If they miss something, read the passage again. If someone states something that isn't in the passage, ask, "Where did you find that in this passage?" Reread the passage, if necessary. (Priesthood of Believers/Group Correction)

- Ask: "What does this passage teach us about God?" (Discovery/Scripture/Priesthood of Believers)

- Ask: "What does this passage teach us about humanity?" (Discovery/Scripture/Priesthood of Believers)

- Ask: "If we believe this passage is from God, how must we change?" (Discovery/Scripture/Obedience/Priesthood of Believers)

- Ask: "Who are you going to share this passage with before we meet again?" (Evangelism/Replication)

🌐 Ask: "When do you want to meet again?" This is a practical question. You will never get someone to commit to a twenty-six-week study. But you can give your group the option to meet again next week. If they are really seeking and if the meeting is filling a need, they will tell you they want to meet again.

You can find the list of Scripture passages we use to disciple lost people into a relationship with Christ in the appendix.

USING GROUPS TO DISCIPLE

We use the pattern we just outlined to disciple and train our leaders—in groups. We select passages from the Bible that address behaviors our leaders need to have (or need to avoid) or things they need to do (or not do) as leaders. When we train leaders, we also ask them to complete a Three-Column Study on the passage—either as a group or as homework before they meet.

OUTLINE OF THE THREE-COLUMN STUDY

Divide a landscape-oriented paper into three columns. Label the first "Scripture." Label the second "My Words" and the third "I Will."

Scripture

The length of the passage you choose affects how much time the study takes. Longer passages take longer to study. This isn't a bad thing, but you need to keep it in mind. Generally, try to keep your passages between ten and fifteen verses.

In the "Scripture" column, write out the passage word for word. This takes time, but you control how much time by choosing smaller chunks of Scripture. Break larger passages into several sections, spread out over several days. What is most important, however, is that when you copy a passage word for word, you actually read it through about five to seven times. It is a form of forced meditation for those of us who can't sit and think about a passage without losing focus. This process also keeps us from skimming familiar passages. When you write it out, you have to think about every word.

My Own Words

When you finish copying the passage, use the second column to write the passage in your own words. Write it out as if you're telling a friend about it over a cup of coffee. Don't move on until you can write the passage in your own words. You see, you don't really understand it if you can't tell it to someone else in your own words. And you can't obey Scripture unless you understand it. It's that simple. Occasionally you may have to stop on a passage for a couple of days and talk it out with the Holy Spirit before you can finish putting it into your own words. When you start this process, you will probably find there are several familiar passages that you can't write in your own words. Sometimes we "know" more than we truly understand.

I Will

In the third column we transition from understanding God's Word to obeying it. Look at each part of the passage. Ask God to reveal things you need to add to your life, take away from your life, or change in your life to obey this passage. Be specific. The passage may say that God created the earth, but you have to decide what that means in your life. How does your life change because you believe God created the earth? What do you need to do differently? What can you do in the next twenty-four hours to obey this passage? Every time we open God's Word, He invites us into relationship. We call His invitation "grace" because we can't do anything to deserve it. Obedience is how we accept His invitation. God lives with those who obey His Word (John 14:23–24). When we study God's Word, we have a choice: we choose to obey Him or we choose to disobey Him. It is really that simple. This third column is your response to God's invitation.

With leaders, we also ask them to apply SPECK to the passage:

S—Is there a **S**in to avoid?

P—Is there a **P**romise, a prayer, or a praise in this passage?

E—Is there an **E**xample to follow (or not follow)?

C—Is there a **C**ommand to obey?

K—Is there **K**nowledge that I need to retain?

Because our leaders came to Christ with their DNA established during the Discovery Group, they easily transition to this pattern as they are discipled as leaders. Furthermore, they naturally use this pattern to train people, and thereby transfer good DNA.

Many people, organizations, and churches believe that starting Discovery Groups alone will allow them to catalyze Disciple-Making Movements in their region. Although Discovery Groups are a powerful tool and transmit much of the DNA required for movement, disciple-makers still need to be committed to being disciples, cultivating lives of prayer, engaging lost communities, and finding Persons of Peace. These things allow you to start groups, but the strategic elements discussed in the next few chapters will help you move from starting groups to catalyzing a movement.

ESTABLISHING CHURCHES

Is an acorn an oak tree? Oak trees produce acorns, but most of us wouldn't say that a mighty oak and such a little nut were the same thing. Yet, that nut has the entire DNA required to become a mighty oak. Sure, the conditions must be right, but every acorn has the potential, the capacity, to be an oak tree. But an acorn isn't an oak tree.

What about a sapling? Sure, a sapling looks more like a tree—kind of. It has leaves and a stem. But depending on the age, it may not have bark yet. Anyone can run over a sapling with their lawn mower, but they can't run over an oak tree. A sapling has more of the characteristics of an oak tree than an acorn, but it's still not an oak tree yet.

Acorns, saplings, and oak trees all have the same DNA. They all require the same conditions to activate their DNA and fulfill their potential. Yet they look nothing alike.

What do you do if you want a one-hundred-year-old oak tree? You plant an acorn in the right soil and, given the right conditions and a hundred years, you'll have a one-hundred-year-old oak tree. Pretty simple, really. Squirrels do the planting. God does the watering. Earthworms take care of the soil.

So, if you want a one-hundred-year-old, mature church in an area, what do you need to do? Pray, engage a community, find Persons of Peace, plant the Gospel through Discovery Groups, baptize people into communities of believers called church, develop leaders, and wait a hundred years. Transplanting a one-hundred-year-old oak tree doesn't make much sense. A transplanted tree will never be as strong as an indigenous one. Rather than starting with the end, we must start at the beginning.

The question, really, is this: At what point does an acorn become an oak tree or a group become a church?

The two of us have been in hundreds of discussions about church over the past forty years, some formal, most informal. There are numerous quagmires in all of these discussions: frequency of meetings; size; leadership; discipline; replication; mission; functions and nature; universal and particular . . . you can add to the list.

All of us tend to define, limit, and project on others our view of church based on our current experiences. We define the acorn and the sapling by the one-hundred-year-old oak trees we love. We want what we are doing to be right, and if we are right, should not everyone be doing church the way we are doing it? But what is right for a new church may be very different from what is right for a century-old church. Of course, this presumes we know the definition of *right*. There are certainly absolutes, but there are also situations where there are seasonal answers/responses.

We all tend to take snapshots of church and define it by that one snapshot. Life is not a snapshot. It's not even a movie. Church is complex and is in constant flux. It has visible aspects, but also invisible aspects. Relationships grow, change, get in trouble, recover (or not), dissolve, and more. It is the nature of organisms to change. Depending on your age, you are not the same person you were fifty, forty, thirty, twenty, or even ten years ago, yet you are the same person. Life changes you, yet you continue to be you. It is not natural to always be the same. But even as we change, we continue to be recognizable.

We often confuse "nature" and "function" of the church. "Nature" cannot be changed. "Function" changes with the needs of the church and the internal/external populations the church serves. The church belonging to Christ is part of the nature of the church. The church gathering is one of the functions. Nature is always true. Function cannot be continuous, but is true at moments. This is the old story of "who we are" and "what we do." Which defines us? Both! When we do something that is contrary to the nature of the church, then who we are is questioned. When we fail to do what our nature would demand, then who we are is questioned. We can occasionally do things that are not related to our nature. We can occasionally not do things our nature would demand. But if we continue to defy our nature, does this not in fact change our nature? And if our nature changes, does this not change who we are? A church that ignores social injustice cannot stay a church regardless of what it calls itself. A church that condones disobedience to God's laws cannot stay a church. A church that does not practice grace and mercy cannot stay a church. It is not easy to be church. We must stand up for what is right, obey all the laws of God, and show grace and mercy in the face of the human condition. How can any human do all this? That's the point. The church is not just human. Is also includes God. This makes it possible to be and do all that is required of church.

We fail to recognize that churches have life cycles, and snapshots during these cycles do not define the whole of what church is. Is a tree seed a tree? Is a sprout a tree? Is a sapling a tree? Is a reproducing tree a tree? Is lumber a tree? When is a tree a tree? If we measure by potential, then the seed or sprout is a tree. If we measure by fruit, then only adult trees are trees. If we measure by value, then tree products and their benefits to us define the tree.

The two of us often get asked for our definition of *church*. It is: "The church is a group of baptized believers in the Lord Jesus Christ who meet regularly to worship, nurture one another (feed and grow one another), and fellowship (practice the "one another" statements of the Bible), and depart these gatherings endeavoring to obey all the commands of Christ in order to transform individuals, families, and communities."

A friend of David's said many years ago, "I can't give you a definition of a church, but when I see one, I know it." Having a good definition of church doesn't mean that a group of people is a church. But somehow we know real church when we see it. This doesn't mean we should not be asking the questions regarding the definition of church. It's healthy to ask the questions. But we must also recognize that any answer to the questions will not be enough of an answer to make "church" happen or determine if "church" is happening. It is the asking of the questions and the discussions these questions raise that help us make sure we are recognized as the church because of whose we are, who we are, and what we do.

Paul called the church "God's household." In 1 Peter 4:17 Christians are referred to as the "family of God." This metaphor of family to describe church has tremendous implications for a community of believers.

Family is the basic building block of society. God established the family at creation. The Bible defines and refines the roles within a family, the position of family within society, and the interactions between families. The relationships found in family are typically deep and complicated. Even dysfunctional families usually have high expectations of roles, identity, acceptance within family, and how the family represents itself to the rest of the community.

Any metaphor breaks down when pushed too far. But metaphors should give meaning and dimension to our understanding. In this case, we need to focus on the ideal concepts related to family and how these relate to a community of believers. None of us will achieve the ideal, but we should strive for it.

Following are some adjectives to help us think about family. These are in no particular order. These descriptors have implications for biological families as well as spiritual families.

- *Generational.* A family is more than father, mother, and children. There are grandparents, great-grandparents, aunts and uncles, cousins, nieces and nephews, grandchildren, great-grandchildren, and more. Some of these relationships are close. Others may even be unknown. But all are family. Families have longer life cycles than individuals.

- *Led.* There are usually one or more elders in charge of the family. Decision making varies, but generally involves a group dynamic with different generations and nearness of relationship having more or less influence on decision making. There is no single way families lead themselves. The very fact that families blend through marriage results in each family being somewhat different from other families, even within the same culture. The way families lead themselves can change, especially when there is traumatic change in leadership. It is also interesting to note that some families lead other families that may not be related to them.

- *Open.* People can marry into family, children may be adopted, and sometimes friends can become like family. In some cultures this openness allows generations to separate into new, distinct family units. In other cultures families can grow to be tight-knit clans that are multigenerational with set hierarchies and succession. There is opportunity for two families to become one blended family in situations where a person who already has children marries another person with children. There may also be times when extreme strife divides a family. Potential new members are scrutinized, but usually become fully associated and identified with the family once integrated.

- *Protective*. Family members look out for one another, watch each other's backs, care for the young and weak, close ranks around those who are unjustly attacked, and stand by those who may be justly attacked, providing appropriate care and nurture. To attack one member of a family is to attack the whole family. In good families this protectiveness promotes growth. Protectiveness allows an environment where the young can grow, and the weak or sick can have opportunity to become stronger.

- *Supportive*. It is expected that family members will support each other emotionally, spiritually, physically, and financially. The level of support given and received is based on need, closeness of relationships, and maturity. In times of crisis roles may reverse, and boundaries that have been set may become more or less restrictive or even disappear.

- *Encouraging*. Good families cheer for one another and help each other reach personal and family goals. They want each member to reach his or her full potential. Love, demonstrated in forgiveness and selflessness, is at the heart of encouragement. The whole family participates in and celebrates the successes of any and every member. Appropriate rivalry and/or competition spur to growth and do not tear down the weak or limit the strong.

🌐 *Identifiable.* People outside the family know who you are because of your family, and what you do reflects positively or negatively on the whole family, not just yourself. Families have names—sometimes good, sometimes bad. Many families have reputations that set positive or negative standards for the community in which they function. Family molds its children to the standards of the family, and may influence communities positively or negatively. Families may have "black-sheep" children or relatives, but these family members are a part of the fabric of the family, and may even be looked upon with pride, depending on what put the black sheep outside the accepted norm for the family. It is generally known who is a part of the family and who is not, by both the family and the community.

🌐 *Reproductive.* One of the purposes of family is to reproduce, multiply, and grow. It is expected that family will be multigenerational. Family lives longer than any single member. It is natural for families to produce multiple branches that may or may not maintain contact with each other.

🌐 *Nurturing.* Families help/encourage/train/educate/mentor one another so that members can reach their own potentials intellectually, physically, emotionally, spiritually, educationally, career-wise, and financially. Leaders are grown. All learn to follow before they lead and as they lead. Teamwork is developed, and individual virtuosity is capitalized for the benefit of the individual and the family.

🌐 *Caring.* People in a family meet each other's needs and the needs of those around them who are not part of the family. Good families do not just look out for themselves and their members, but for the community at large, and perhaps for people they have never met. Care is expressed in generosity to those in need, regardless of background or family membership. Care for family members will come first, but is not exclusive. When neighbors or strangers are in need, then families that care for one another will turn that care toward others. Families that care for each other give care to others.

- *Mobile*. No family is found in only one place. Some families divide and move because of circumstances. Other families plan their divisions and movements. Families survive by planting themselves in many places.

- *Versatile*. Though families are often identified as being part of one community or one profession, this is not usually the reality of any family. Most families are highly diversified. Successful families are always diversified in educational backgrounds, occupational backgrounds, political affiliation, and sometimes nationality. Versatility promotes survivability. Changing with the times assures the family's future, just as heritage provides stability for the family. Innovation and tradition are required for true versatility. Tradition provides the stability and platform for innovation. Innovation keeps tradition from becoming petrified and limiting. Great tradition is based on principles that propel the family into the future. What has been becomes greater through innovation. The nature of God is creative. He bestowed that nature on humankind. To deny innovation is to deny the very nature of God. Families need traditions that promote creative initiatives. Families need innovation in order to remain viable and healthy.

● *Loving.* Family members put one another before self. They expect and wish the best for one another. They make the best happen for one another when and if possible. They accept what cannot be changed and change what must be changed. They give grace to those who fall, picking them up when they do. Healthy families forgive, and members are forgiven when they fail. Families hope for improvement, and strive to make it happen. They remember the good, learn from mistakes, and forget the bad. Family members bless one another and are a blessing to each other. They are the stepping-stone to success for each other, and give a hand up to others when they become successful. Families help the weaker members and heal the sick. They sacrifice so that others may grow, benefit, and succeed. Open to strangers and yet fiercely protective, families are caring and nurturing. Family members give their lives so that others, or another, may live. Families give all they know, that others may grow. They are generous, recognizing growth, success, character, generosity, achievement, and sacrifice. Families strive for humility and excellence. They are always learning and teaching, always serving, always loving.

All of these have overwhelming implications for a community of believers. This is the kind of church a contagious disciple-maker wants to be part of and plant. These are the kinds of churches contagious disciple-makers want to grow.

The following passages address all the core parts of being a family of believers.

COMMANDS FOR LIVING IN COMMUNITY
("ONE ANOTHER" PASSAGES)

1. Accept one another. (Rom 15:7)
2. Agree with one another. (1 Cor. 1:10; Phil. 4:2)
3. Bear with one another. (Col. 3:13)
4. Remember that we belong to one another. (Rom.12:5)
5. Consider one another as better. (Phil. 2:3)
6. Do not break faith with one another. (Mal. 2:10)
7. Build up one another. (Eph. 4:29; 1 Thess. 5:11)
8. Do not be a burden to one another. (Gal. 6:4–5)
9. Carry one another's burdens. (Gal. 6:2)
10. Do not compare yourselves to one another. (Gal. 6:4–5)
11. Have equal concern for one another. (1 Cor. 12:25–27)
12. Confess your sins to one another. (James 5:16)
13. Do not covet one another's spouses. (Ex. 20:17; Deut. 5:21)
14. Do not desire one another's property. (Ex. 20:17; Deut. 5:21)
15. Let no debt remain outstanding to one another. (Rom. 13:8)
16. Do not allow stealing, lying, and deception to be a part of your relationships with one another. (Lev. 19:11)
17. Do not devour or destroy one another. (Gal. 5:15)
18. Be devoted to one another. (Rom. 12:10)
19. Discipline one another. (Matt. 18:15–17)
20. Do good and share with one another. (Heb. 13:16)
21. Build up one another with your faith. (Rom. 1:11–12)
22. Encourage one another. (1 Thess. 4:18; 5:11; Titus 1:9; Heb. 3:13; 10:25)
23. Spur one another on toward love and good deeds. (Heb. 10:24)

24. Do not envy one another. (Gal. 5:26)

25. Judge one another fairly. (Lev. 19:15)

26. Do not do anything to cause one another to fall. (Rom. 14:21)

27. Fellowship with one another. (1 John 1:7)

28. Forgive one another. (Matt.18:21–35; Eph. 4:32; Col. 3:13)

29. Serve one another with your gifts. (1 Cor. 12:7; 1 Peter 4:10)

30. Give to one another. (Prov. 3:28; Luke 6:30; 17:3–4)

31. Greet one another. (Rom. 16:16; 1 Peter 5:14)

32. Do not hold a grudge against one another. (Lev. 19:18)

33. Do not grumble against one another. (James 5:9)

34. Do not be hardhearted or tightfisted toward one another. (Deut. 15:7)

35. Do not plot harm against one another. (Prov. 3:29)

36. Live in harmony with one another. (Rom. 12:16; 1 Peter 3:8)

37. Do not hate one another in your hearts. (Lev. 19:17)

38. Honor one another above yourselves. (Rom. 12:10)

39. Offer hospitality to one another without grumbling. (1 Peter 4:9)

40. Have humility toward one another. (1 Peter 5:5)

41. Do not do things that will hurt one another. (Rom. 14:15)

42. Be full of goodness, complete in knowledge, and competent to instruct one another. (Rom. 15:14)

43. Do not charge one another interest on personal loans of money or goods. (Deut. 23:19)

44. Do not judge one another. (Rom. 14:10, 13; 14:13; James 4:12)

45. Be kind to one another and everyone else. (1 Thess. 5:15; 2 Tim. 2:24; Eph. 4:32)

46. Do not lie to or about one another. (Ex. 20:16; Deut. 5:20; Col. 3:9–10)

47. Look after one another's interests. (Phil. 2:4)

48. Do not gloat over the destruction of one another, or boast about your good fortune when others are in trouble. (Obad. 1:12)

49. Do not look down on one another. (Rom. 14:10)

50. Love one another. (Lev. 19:18; Matt. 22:36–39; Mark 12:28–31; Luke 10:25–27; John 13:34–35; 15:12; 17; Rom. 13:9; Gal. 5:14; 1 Thess. 3:12; 4:9; 2 Thess. 1:3; Heb. 13:1; James 2:8; 1 Peter 1:22; 4:8; 1 John 3:11, 23; 4:7, 11–12; 2 John 1:5–6; see also 1 Corinthians 13:4–13)

51. Have mercy and compassion for one another. (Zech. 7:9)

52. Be openhanded with one another. (Deut. 15:11)

53. Be patient with one another. (Eph. 4:2)

54. Be at peace with one another. (Mark 9:50; 1 Thess. 5:12–13)

55. Pray for one another. (James 5:16)

56. Do not provoke one another. (Gal. 5:26)

57. Rebuke one another so you don't share another's guilt. (Lev. 19:17)

58. Be reconciled to one another. (Matt. 5:23–24)

59. Show respect to one another. (1 Peter 2:17)

60. Gently restore one another when caught in sin. (Gal. 6:1)

61. Do not seek revenge against one another. (Lev. 19:18)

62. Seek the good of one another. (1 Cor. 10:24)

63. Serve one another. (Gal. 5:13)

64. Do not slander one another. (James 4:11)

65. Speak to one another with psalms, hymns and spiritual songs. (Eph. 5:19–20)

66. Do not steal from one another by stealth, force, trickery or deceit. (Lev. 19:13)

67. Do not put stumbling blocks or obstacles in one another's way. (Rom. 14:13)

68. Submit to one another. (1 Cor. 16:15–16; Eph. 5:21)

69. Do not take advantage of one another. (Lev. 25:14, 17)

70. Teach and admonish one another. (Col. 3:16)

71. Make sure there is a good reason to testify against one another. (Prov. 24:28)

72. Do not think evil of one another. (Zech. 7:10)

73. Speak truth to one another. (Zech. 8:16–17)

74. Do not plot evil against one another. (Zech. 8:16–17)

75. Wait for one another. (1 Cor. 11:33)

HELPING A GROUP TRANSITION TO CHURCH

Helping groups make the transition to become these kinds of families, these kinds of churches, takes time and effort. The disciple-maker coaches the Person of Peace and/or spiritual leaders of the group every week for months on how to lead a Discovery Group focused on discovering God. This series of Bible studies addresses the group's worldview and cultural gateways and barriers. It leads them to discover a holy and loving God, face their own sin, find God's provision for their sin through Jesus Christ, come into a grace/faith relationship with Jesus, and commit to a life of faith that obeys His commands regardless of consequences. At some point in this process the group comes to Christ, often all at one time or over a short period of time. They are baptized as they discover and obey the biblical teachings on belief in Christ and baptism, and begin the process of moving from being a Bible study group to being a church.

During this process the disciple-maker spent anywhere from six months to two years coaching and mentoring the Person of Peace and/or the spiritual leaders of the affinity group. He will spend about another two years mentoring the leaders of this new group to help them fully develop as a church. This may not be the only group the disciple-maker works with, and each group, most likely, is at different stages of the disciple-making process.

As the group transitions from being a Discovery Group to being church, the discovery process becomes routine, requiring less time and energy on the disciple-maker's part. He simply introduces new Scripture passages, answers questions, and continues building relationships with the leaders of the group. But when the group is about to come to Christ, spiritual warfare heats up, while time and relationship requirements increase. This is often a crisis point in the relationships, and much prayer and more time is needed to usher the leaders and the group through this critical passage. The disciple-maker may be tempted to take control of the group—but shouldn't. He or she must continue to coach and mentor the leaders, allowing the Holy Spirit to usher them into the presence of the King. As a result, the disciple-maker will experience the joy that comes with the birth of a new church.

Now the disciple-maker's job changes from being the midwife, who assisted the Holy Spirit in the birth of a church, to the nanny, who helps the church reach maturity. Notice that the nanny is not the parent, but assists the parent in helping the child to mature to responsible adulthood. Though giving birth seems like hard work, those of us who have raised children to adulthood know that the hardest part of being a parent lies ahead as we raise the children to responsible adulthood. The work of the disciple-maker increases greatly as the new church begins its walk to maturity.

The amount of time spent mentoring the new church leaders increases dramatically for a few months. There is a lot to learn from the Word in order for the leaders to understand and fulfill their responsibilities as leaders. They also may already be involved in starting other groups or even have other groups coming to their own crisis point of becoming a new church. There is a great temptation on behalf of the disciple-maker to become a directive leader and/or teacher at this point. There is so much that needs to be done, so much that these leaders need to know, so many issues that have to be addressed, that the disciple-maker feels compelled to sit them down and inundate them with knowledge. Disciple-makers must resist this temptation!

At this stage you, as the disciple-maker, should increase your time with Discovery Group leaders by 50 to 100 percent by spending time with them outside the Discovery Group. Let what they experience guide you in what Scripture passages you introduce them to through the Discovery Group process. Let the Word teach them and let them take this process to their groups. Go through the life and commands of Jesus. Help these new leaders learn to lead from Jesus and Paul by not just asking what they taught, but looking at what they did with their disciples. Explore Scripture together, focusing on the function, nature, and leadership of the church. Let the Word and the Holy Spirit guide the group to finding their own fulfillment as the Bride of Christ, the Body of Christ, and the Pillar and Foundation of Truth for their communities. Help them look with new eyes on their family, friends, and neighbors in order to love them more and seek ways to serve them and meet their needs. Brainstorm with these new leaders how to meet the needs of those around them out of their own resources. Explore ways to develop local resources. Don't do anything to develop dependence on outside assistance for anything.

As you put these patterns in place with love and devotion, you will see a responsible church emerge that will transform its own community and reach out to all segments of society around it. It will look over the horizon to other communities who need what they have found. It will become a reproducing, responsible church led by reproducing, responsible leaders who equip reproducing, responsible disciples for Jesus Christ.

17

LEADERSHIP

"Good-bye" does not mean relationships are over. It means they have changed. When a parent says good-bye to a kindergarten child on the very first day of school, the parenting relationship changes but does not end. When a mom and dad say good-bye to a son or daughter who is off to college for the first time, the relationship changes. When parents say good-bye to a son or daughter at the altar of marriage, the relationship changes. If the parent does not say good-bye, severe damage occurs, not only for the relationship, but also for the development of the child into a responsible adult.

Jesus said in John 16:7, "But I tell you the truth: It is for your good that I am going away. Unless I go away, the Counselor will not come to you; but if I go, I will send him to you." Jesus was limited by time and space. If He had not ascended, we would have limited access to the knowledge and power of God through Jesus. The Holy Spirit is not limited by time or space or in the number of people who can access Him. Jesus' followers can accomplish much more since Jesus ascended than we could have if He had stayed on the earth. The Holy Spirit provides for everyone to access to the love of God, His power, His wisdom, and His understanding of the Word.

New churches have a very high dependence on the disciple-maker. If the disciple-maker stays too long, then he or she will cripple the growth of the new church. Instead of learning to depend on the Holy Spirit and the Word of God for guidance, the church will depend on the disciple-maker. This is unhealthy. It severely limits a church's potential, and in the worst cases can kill a new church before it even has a chance to develop.

Disciple-makers need to prepare the churches they start for the time of separation. This is done by continually going to the Bible for answers to all questions. It is done through prayer and seeing that God answers the new believer's prayers. This preparation comes through equipping leadership and letting that leadership lead from the very beginning as they listen to the Holy Spirit and depend on the Word of God for guidance.

If the disciple-maker stays too long, he runs the danger of taking the place of the Holy Spirit in the life of the church. It will be the disciple-maker who points out sin instead of the Holy Spirit convicting of sin as God's Word reveals it. It will be the disciple-maker who answers the church's prayers by providing advice and assistance instead of the Holy Spirit providing all their needs. When there are problems and persecutions, the church will turn to the disciple-maker instead of God for solutions and salvation.

If the disciple-maker has done his or her job, then the church has seen the disciple-maker model a mature Christian lifestyle and leadership. The disciple-maker equipped the church to handle God's Word, pray and listen to the Spirit of God, and minister to the people around them. As leaders emerge in the new church, the disciple-maker watches them lead and mature, observes their mistakes, and helps them recover from mistakes by listening to the Word of God and His Spirit. And at the right time the disciple-maker leaves, knowing that the church is in good hands, the hands of the Holy Spirit.

Know when it's time to say good-bye. It's not the end of the relationship but the start of a new and better one. The disciple-making relationship is about leadership development. The remainder of this book focuses on leadership development and mentoring within the context of making contagious disciples and catalyzing Disciple-Making Movements.

THE LONG TAIL OF LEADERSHIP

The "Long Tail" is a statistical concept used to illustrate a specific distribution of numbers along a graph that looks like a long tail. Chris Anderson wrote a book called *The Long Tail: Why the Future of Business Is Selling Less of More* (New York: Hyperion, 2006), in which he applied this statistical principle to illustrate a phenomenon online where total sales of almost unknown books or albums actually equal or surpass total sales by blockbusters in their field. Merchants like Amazon and iTunes aren't limited by geography and shelf space, so they can afford to host books, albums, or songs that only sell a couple of copies a year. When you aggregate the total sales of albums and books that may only sell up to twenty copies in a year, they exceed the sales of the blockbusters.

APPLYING THE LONG TAIL TO LEADERSHIP

After talking about Chris's book and looking into the statistical concept of the Long Tail, we realized it can be used to illustrate an important leadership concept. In the following graph, "Leadership Capacity" refers to the number of people or tribes a person leads. "Number of Leaders" refers to the number of people who can lead. This adjusted graph, "The Long Tail of Leadership," captures the idea that few people have the capacity to lead large groups of people, and a great number of people have the capacity to lead groups as small as three to five people. People like Rick Warren, for example, have the capacity to lead several thousand, while your average disciple-maker may only have the capacity to lead ten or so.

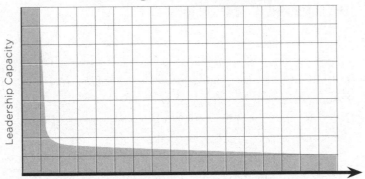

The Long Tail of Leadership

Leadership Capacity

Number of Leaders

TWO APPROACHES TO LEADERSHIP DEVELOPMENT

You can look for leaders with the potential to be in the short head of the Long Tail of Leadership, load them up with education and training, and hope they can knock one out of the park. They look good, and your organization benefits. But if all your eggs are in this one basket, the organization's success rises and falls on these super-leaders. Most MBA programs try to develop these super-leaders. Seminaries try to as well.

Or you can find leaders in the mid to lower tail and help them lead their families, communities, and silos. If you help them enough, your relationship becomes influence. Influence is the most effective currency any leader has. If you influence enough leaders in the long tail, you actually end up leading more people than most super-leaders. This way, your eggs aren't all in one basket—at least as far as leadership is concerned. If one leader self-destructs, his or her community replaces them.

Think about it this way. It takes a high-capacity leader to create a silo from a group of non-related individuals. Pastors and traditional church planters do this all the time. Their jobs require high levels of natural capacity and training. In fact, most pastors have six to eight years of training and experience. In this paradigm, leadership development is pretty long. If you leverage the leadership within existing silos, however, you cut leadership development time and cost by more than half because you don't expect them to lead total strangers. Instead, you help them lead their existing families, communities, and silos more effectively.

As people effectively lead their existing community, those with the capacity to lead larger communities will do so. Those with the capacity to lead multiple communities within their silo will do that as well. If you watch for these emerging leaders and mentor them as they develop, you have a better chance to develop leaders who do great things rather than nonleaders, or not-yet-leaders, who merely think they are great.

Every city is full of existing silos containing communities, families, and affinity groups with existing leadership. Help those leaders lead their tribes and you will develop the influence necessary to change a lot of lives. Of course, you have to really want to help people, or they will see through you in a moment, and you will lose any hope of making a difference beyond your own community and silo.

LEADING THROUGH INFLUENCE

As far as we know, Disciple-Making Movements are the only modern example of the Gospel spreading rapidly throughout decentralized systems. All leaders of active Disciple-Making

Movements around the world lead by influence rather than position. This is a strong indicator of the leadership style necessary for catalyzing Disciple-Making Movements in the United States and other locations around the world. People who want to catalyze Disciple-Making Movements must become master influencers of multiple systems to achieve the end goal of reaching their family, community, silo, city, and nation. People who lead by influence have five characteristics.

1. Influential leaders are valuable to different networks at different levels.

   I (Paul) grew up watching leaders and emerging leaders of Disciple-Making Movements. I've seen them lead high-level meetings, and I've seen them have lunch with brand-new church planters. I've watched them make decisions that involve several partners working toward a common goal, and I've watched them sit in a room, listening to the stories of five men who just want to save their people with the Gospel. In each case, leaders worked to help each network—big and small—think through what was necessary for them to reach their people with the Gospel. Their official role in the discussions didn't matter; in every case, the influential leader led from the position he or she was given at that moment in time. Consequently, these leaders became valuable to many networks, on many levels, and helped them accomplish great things over time.

2. Influential leaders become successful when they help others become successful.

   Influential leaders do not consider themselves successful until the people they lead and mentor are successful. In terms of replication, leaders in Disciple-Making Movements are not successful until the individuals they are discipling are each discipling someone else. Influential leaders do not have to be on stage, receiving accolades. Instead, they get tremendous pleasure out of seeing someone they've mentored being recognized for their hard work and success.

3. Influential leaders have the ability to accurately assess the situation and adapt on the fly.

Many meetings start with one purpose and end having accomplished something completely different! Good influential leaders are masters of reading situations and quickly adjusting their approach. They don't allow themselves to get flustered by sudden and unforeseen change. I was actually in the room once when this happened. I watched them mentally step back, reassess, and ask questions that helped them get a better picture of what was going on. Once they understood the currents in the room, they got the conversation moving by suggesting alternative approaches or throwing out ideas for group consideration.

4. Influential leaders establish high levels of relational accountability.

This point is really hard to picture, especially if you've been the victim of domineering and unpleasant accountability systems. These relationships look different depending on the network and role the leader has within that network. Wise leaders focus on accountability to obey God's Word and encourage replication in all areas.

This kind of accountability is best framed by the following questions:

- What are you learning from God's Word?
- How are you applying it within your network?

- Whom are you discipling?
- Whom are they discipling?
- How can I help?

5. Influential leaders have the ability to compartmentalize.

Since they work across multiple networks, and in different capacities within those networks, influential leaders have the ability to focus on the network at hand. They cannot allow relationships with other people and networks to unduly influence their role in the network they are in at the moment. They must maintain confidences across networks. They accept a lesser role in one network even while they have a higher role in another. They have to remember their role in each network and function within that role while they are in that network. To top it off, they have to remember the ultimate goal of their activity in multiple networks—to catalyze Disciple-Making Movements that result in millions (not an exaggeration!) coming to know Christ as their Lord and Savior.

THE DIFFERENCE BETWEEN LEADERSHIP AND MANAGEMENT

Most of us have spent a lifetime studying leadership. We have read all the secular and religious leadership and management books we can get our hands on. We have attended the conferences and seminars, and some of us have led conferences or seminars on leadership. Many of us have degrees that include elements of management and/or leadership. Our ministries are about developing leaders, and we are serious about our coaching and mentoring skills.

With all this information, why is it that there is a lack of good leaders, much less great leaders, in the world—whether we are looking at government, business, nonprofits, or ministry? Understand, we are not talking about management but about leadership. For many, there is little difference between management and leadership. Both involve people. Both are about reaching objectives. But the focus is very different. Management requires some leadership skills, and leadership certainly requires some management skills.

Management is about the task, getting results, reaching the goals, fulfilling the mission, and resources required to fulfill the vision. Leadership is about people. In management, good people skills and management skills help make these objectives happen. But it's a matter of focusing on the task, the results, and the mission. People are a resource in the mix and, for some, a necessary evil. Many managers look for ways to limit the human variable in the equation. We all know that the weakest link in all management systems is the people. They have different capacities, different skill sets, different temperaments and personalities. Some are fun; some are not. Some work hard, some don't. We study ways to get the most out of people, and then wonder why there are always those we can't seem to engage or motivate to help us reach our goals, to be successful.

But leadership is about helping people reach their capacity as individuals and as teams, and even exceeding personal capacity through hard work, desire, and team building. Leadership is more than good people skills and good management skills. It is about helping people find what they are good at and then helping them become the best at what they do. Leadership is about getting people in the right place at the right time, with the right knowledge and skills and the right attitudes, so they can succeed. The by-product of their success is mission accomplished and people who will reproduce themselves into others, thus producing more people who will accomplish the mission.

Management is about the details and resources required to fulfill the vision. Don't misunderstand: We need great managers. But great managers without great leadership rarely succeed because managers don't draw people to them. Leaders, on the other hand, always draw others into their circles of influence and management. Managers often have to recruit people. Leaders select people from those who are coming around them as a result of their leadership lifestyles.

But leadership is about understanding and having a vision and having the capacity to help others move from not understanding the vision to adopting the vision. As evangelists for the vision, leaders help people move from not knowing how to accomplish the vision to taking the steps necessary to fulfill the vision. Leaders help people move from doubting themselves to having confidence in leading others.

Managers measure success in terms of tasks and the resources required to accomplish those tasks. They are good at bringing resources, including people, to bear on a task or problem and achieving a positive outcome, however the organization defines "positive." Successful management is the minimum use of resources to accomplish the tasks; the margin between expenditure of resources and the gain from accomplishing the task is often the measure of good management. In other words, management produces a product that is counted as a positive outcome for the organization. For a business, this is money. For a school, it is successful graduates. For a ministry, it is people served. For a politician or political party, it is gaining and keeping office. For a club, it is getting others to adopt the club's values and promote them to others.

But leadership measures success in terms of people development. Leaders spot people with capacity and help them reach it, and even exceed it. Often, great leaders produce other leaders who will be even greater than they are. Great leaders bring together teams of potential leaders who complement and sharpen one another. Good leaders have the ability to bring together teams who accomplish more together than any of them produce individually. In the process, each member of the team learns and develops because of exposure to others and because of an environment that encourages learners to develop into leaders.

Spotting great managers is easy. They produce, and the results are visible in the bottom line. That bottom line may be widgets produced, people served, profit made, or organizational growth.

Spotting great leaders is more difficult. Look for people who spot other people who are diamonds in the rough, and through tough love, hard work, and encouragement produce polished leaders who are recognized for their leadership and management skills. For great leaders, glory is in others' successes, not in being recognized personally. Great leaders don't have to be the "boss" in order to accomplish the mission. They work through influence, and usually lead "up" (lead those who have managerial responsibility for them as a resource to the organization).

Managers often insist that things have to be done a certain way. They are always concerned with procedures. Managers focus on efficient systems and processes that minimize mistakes and maximize the bottom line.

But great leaders develop through a learning process that minimizes the repetition of mistakes. They do this by focusing not on mistakes but on what can be learned from mistakes so that they are not made again. Great leaders are learners who have the ability to motivate others to become learners. Learners are active and go after information and skills to fill their capacity, while students are passive and wait for situations or others to force them to learn. Students rarely reach capacity, while learners often find ways to increase their capacity.

WHAT ARE LEADERS MADE OF?

I (David) have been in the business of identifying and equipping leaders for more than thirty years. For most of this time I really did not feel qualified to judge if a person would become a good leader or not. From experience, I know that some people who look as though they could be good leaders never develop into leaders. I have also seen people who were passed over time after time for leadership responsibility, but when they were finally given a chance to lead, blossomed into tremendous leaders. First impressions do not define a leader.

Many today state categorically that leadership is about character. Indeed, character is certainly an essential element for Christian leaders. Yet all of us know leaders who do not demonstrate good character, as well as people with great character who cannot lead. Do not misunderstand: leaders should have exemplary character. But character alone does not define a leader.

Some would like to think training and education can make a good leader, but this is not true. Training and education give a leader the tools necessary to move to a new level of leadership. However, we know extremely competent leaders who are illiterate, yet capable of leading thousands of people. So, training and education do not define a leader.

Another school of thought insists great leaders are born to lead. This implies that leadership is genetic, and only a select few will ever excel in leadership. If this is true, the world is in trouble. We need millions of leaders in all areas of life. If leaders are born to lead, then there will be no way to plan for the future and no way to really identify potential leaders. Birthright does not make a leader.

So, what does define a leader? Is there a formula to follow that will always produce good leaders? No, there isn't a formula, but there is a prescription. Paul identified it in 2 Timothy 2:2: "And the things you have heard me say in the presence of many witnesses entrust to reliable men who will also be qualified to teach others."

Real leaders produce more leaders. They identify reliable people to whom they pass on what they've learned. These reliable people are qualified to teach others. And in turn, these reliable people look for more reliable people to equip to be the next generation of leaders.

The following are the qualities that identify a potential leader:

1. They are learners. Learners are people who continuously get what they need in order to do what needs to be done.

2. They know how to delegate. Delegators recognize that every worthwhile job requires a team to complete, and they understand that the best way to equip others for a job is to show them how to do the job, let them do it, and insist that they teach others to do the job. Great delegators know how to take their hands off in order to create a leadership vacuum that potential leaders will fill if given the chance.

3. They are good judges of character. Character is judged by what a person does, not by what is said. Reliable people always do what they say, and what they say is good and right. Good character is a result of practiced obedience to the Word of God.

4. They choose the right people to equip (who will also be qualified to teach others). Equippers spend their time and energy on people who will be able to equip others.

When qualifying a person for leadership, we want to know some things about her.

1. What is she currently learning in order to get a job done?

2. Is the job she is doing big enough to require a team, and if so, how did she choose the team and how is she equipping the team?

3. Are stated beliefs and values demonstrated in personal action? Does she do what she says?

4. Are the people she chooses to equip engaged in equipping others?

Real leaders are reliable people who demonstrate good character and learn what they need to accomplish and what must be done so they can engage others in a worthy cause in a manner that results in new, self-replicating leaders.

MADE PERFECT IN WEAKNESS

One of the frequent sayings in leadership seminars regarding teams is, "You are only as strong as your weakest member." This statement is even heard at Christian leadership conferences. This may appear to be true in business-related teams and sports teams, but from biblical and ministry teaming perspectives, this statement falls short of reality. All teams are only as strong as their ability to work with their weakest member(s) and see success. This applies even when every team member is highly qualified, well prepared, and extremely motivated.

In military conflict or operations, a man may become injured and ineffective. Consequently, he is a weak link. The true test of a team is not that it has no weak links, but that even when it has weak links, it can still stay on mission and succeed. "No man left behind" is not just a statement. It is a commitment to those who have become weak to finish the task and get them home regardless of circumstances. This builds *esprit de corps* and allows men and women to perform incredible feats in the face of death or tremendous opposition.

Some say the military weeds out the weak. This is not the case. The military allows everyone to strive for strength, and those who make it protect our shores and serve our nation. They should not be forgotten or ignored when they have fallen or become weak in the performance of their duties. Forgetting the weak is the path to weakness.

There are certainly circumstances where individuals have no capacity to become strong. In these situations such individuals must accept opportunities for other life ventures that provide the possibility of success related to teams with different requirements.

As team leaders, we recruit and build our teams based on our weaknesses, not our strengths. If we look for people just like us, then we will all be weak in the same area and ensure failure. By knowing our weaknesses and recruiting team members who have strengths where we are weak, we ensure the potential success of the team.

Successful business teams require people with different strengths. Not all can be accountants or marketing experts or engineers or designers. By definition this means they are weak in other areas of business. Even if you are working with the top ten in every field of endeavor, there will be unseen and unknown weaknesses that the team must adapt to in order to see success.

Any successful sports team has members who are strong in certain areas of the sport. This means they are probably weak in other areas. Most baseball pitchers are not strong hitters. Most quarterbacks are not strong blockers. Most basketball centers don't shoot well from three-point range. And even All-Star teams lose games. Look at the 2004 USA Olympic basketball team, who lost more games in a single year than all other USA Olympic basketball teams in history combined.

Teaming is about more than the strengths of the team members. It is about how the team members support one another's weaknesses so the team will be strong.

From a biblical perspective there are several counterintuitives when compared to modern teaming concepts:

We need the weak. (See 1 Corinthians 12:12–30.) I have learned more life lessons in hospitals, nursing homes, homes for people with handicaps, and working with so-called disadvantaged people, than I ever learned in the high-powered business meeting, gym, or sporting event. We become more creative when we work around weaknesses in ourselves and/or team members. We get the opportunity to see life from a different perspective and solve problems when making concessions to any weakness.

Christ's power is made perfect in weakness. (See 2 Corinthians 12:9–10.) Without the weak or our own weaknesses, we are unable to see the power of Christ. It is in the weak and in our own weaknesses that we have the opportunity to see Christ show up and make a difference when we could not. Success in the face of weakness makes it clear that we are not responsible for the ultimate outcome.

God chose to reveal Himself in the weak things of the earth. (See 1 Corinthians 1:27–29.) So that we cannot boast, God chose to work through the weak things of the earth. This shames the strong, meaning that no one is strong enough to live without God. When we exclude the weak from our teams, we exclude the way God works from our teams. Some will say, "But we are all weak." This is true, but how often do we act as if we are weak and acknowledge that God works through our weaknesses?

We are responsible to help the weak. (See 1 Thessalonians 5:14.) We should not cast the weak out or ignore the weak. We help the weak. How can we expect others to develop if we exclude them because they don't measure up to our standards of strength? How often have we seen people who were rejected in their early lives become incredible leaders as they mature? How often do we step around fallen, weak brothers and sisters as we go on about our business? We have a responsibility to incorporate those who are weaker on our teams in order to help them grow. This is not easy but can be fulfilling for all if we assign tasks to the weaker person that he or she can handle, and listen to his or her perspective that may be closer to those we are trying to serve. Teams don't exist for the sake of themselves. They exist to do God's will, accomplish tasks, and expand the Kingdom of God.

We are to bear the failings of the weak. (See Romans 15:1.) The only way we can bear the failings of the weak is to include them on our teams. The moment we exclude them, force them away from us, or simply ignore them, we make it impossible to bear their failings. What is interesting is that we become failures in love and obedience when we behave this way.

Disciple-making teams must not be built on the philosophies of the business world. Our teams must be built on biblical principles that build up the body of Christ, the team, and each team member. How we do things is at least as important as what we do. Unbiblical, immoral, unethical practices make us a failure even if we succeed by worldly standards.

We must not forget who we are, and whose we are.

MEASURING THE RIGHT THINGS

Many leaders only measure what communicates success internally and externally. Communicating internal success builds morale by letting people know they accomplished what the organization wants. Communicating external success builds the loyalty of constituents and donors, thus keeping the organization alive. Internal and external successes are certainly strategic. Strategic elements are those that, when broken or absent, cause the strategy to significantly falter or fail. So, both internal and external successes can be strategic, but they are not the only strategic elements. You can have the best and happiest workers and all the money in the world, but if you don't have the right leaders with the right plans doing the right things at the right time in the right way for the right reasons, the strategy will fail, unless your strategy is to keep workers and donors happy regardless of whether Kingdom purposes are met.

In most complex strategies, there are numerous strategic elements. In Contagious Disciple-Making that results in self-replicating disciples, leaders, groups, and churches that take seriously the Great Commandment and the Great Commission, these strategic or critical elements fall into three groups: *Kingdom elements*, *tactical elements*, and *leadership elements*. This book focuses on the seven strategic elements and subsequent tactics necessary to start a Disciple-Making Movement. The following is a more complete list of the strategic elements used to start and sustain a Disciple-Making Movement. If any of them are missing, there will be serious difficulties fulfilling kingdom purposes.

Kingdom elements include the following:

- Prayer: Pervasive prayer is the starting point for all ministry. We must know the mind of God and join Him in His work.

- Scripture: Scripture is foundational and the source of all teaching and preaching. Scripture leads to principles, which lead to practice.

- Disciples: Make disciples, not converts. Converts focus on religion. Disciples focus on Jesus and obedience to His teachings.

- Obedience: Teach obedience to the Word, not doctrine. Doctrine is our church's teaching from the Bible as well as the historical practices of the church. It may be highly interpretive, and may not consider the full counsel of the Bible.

- Communities of Believers (church): Form new believers into Discovery Groups with as few extrabiblical practices and beliefs as possible so that they become Communities of Believers (churches) who transform families and communities.

- Authority of the Word and the Holy Spirit: Authority of Scripture and the Holy Spirit are all that is needed to establish self-replicating disciples, leaders, and churches. Church planting is an act of God through His Spirit and His people who are obedient to the Word and the Spirit.

- Persecution: Persecution is part of being a Christian. In pioneer work it is expected and response is trained.

- Spiritual warfare: In areas where the Gospel has never been preached, or in areas where traditional religions have reigned for a significant amount of time, it is not unusual to find those engaging in DMM activities confronted by spiritual conflicts that range from annoying to life-threatening.

- Sacrifice: Disciple-makers must be prepared to sacrifice security and comforts to fulfill the Great Commandment and Great Commission.

Tactical elements include the following:

- Groups: Groups/communities learn more quickly, remember more things and remember them better, replicate more quickly, and when correctly established, protect against heresy and bad leadership.

- Planning/being intentional: Plan your work and work your plan. Be intentional in ministry, prayer, Scripture, and disciple-making.

- Engagement: Service, also called ministry, opens the door for disciple-making and leads to community transformation as the church obeys the ministry commands of Scripture. Ministry precedes evangelism, and evangelism is always the desired result of ministry. Timing is important and necessary, especially in highly resistant societies.

- Persons of Peace: Start with the Person of Peace or an existing relationship that will permit a Discovery Group or witness.

- Households/families/affinity groups: Focus on households/families/affinity groups, not individuals. Households include non-related people living and relating together as family.

- Evangelism: Evangelism is the act of inviting a Person of Peace and his or her family/household/affinity group to study God's Word in order to move from not knowing God to falling in love with Him through Jesus. Disciple-makers extend the Kingdom of God through evangelism. The primary method used is the Discovery Group in relationship with maturing believers. This makes disciples, not converts.

- Reproducing: Reproducing disciples, leaders, groups, and churches becomes a part of the group DNA.

- Reaching out (missions): Reaching out to all segments of society becomes a part of the group DNA as a result of obedience to the Great Commission (missions) and the Great Commandments.

- Redeeming local culture (embracing the local culture): Do not import external culture, but redeem local culture by embracing all you biblically can in a culture and allowing obedience to the Word to transform/redeem the rest.

Leadership elements include the following:

- Inside leaders: Keep all things reproducible by inside leaders and directed/led by inside leaders.

- Outside leaders: Outside leaders model, equip, watch, and leave. Outside leaders introduce new concepts that are contextualized by inside leaders. Outside leaders deculturalize; inside leaders contextualize.

- Self-supporting leaders: Self-supporting, local leaders start and sustain all work—including groups, fellowships, and churches. Self-supporting may mean the worker has a job or business. This improves access and breaks down the unbiblical barriers between clergy and laity.

- Education: Education increases knowledge through teaching. The focus is on knowledge.

- Training: Training increases skill sets primarily through coaching. The focus is on the task and behaviors or character of the workers.

- Equipping: Equipping increases capacity through mentoring relationships. The focus is on the person, helping individuals become all that God has called them to be.

We have to make sure that our metrics measure the things that get us to Kingdom success in our strategic elements. Determining and evaluating what you measure really gets you where you want to go. Your teams do what you measure. So, if you measure what does not get you to Kingdom purposes, you will never reach Kingdom goals.

Most organizations only measure quantitative goals. Quantitative goals are easy to count: number of Bibles distributed, number of Bible studies started, number of people evangelized, number of converts, number of baptisms, number of new churches, number of new places entered, number of leaders trained, and so forth. If you can count it, it's most likely a quantitative goal.

Not all Kingdom goals can be counted, though. Some are qualitative. Discipleship is a qualitative goal—hard to count, but absolutely essential to reaching Kingdom goals. Obedience is a qualitative goal. These, and others, are important and essential to reaching Kingdom goals.

Kingdom Metrics

Kingdom metrics are what we use to measure our work by God's expectations, as He revealed them in Scripture. Kingdom metrics help us understand how God measures what we do, which allows us to develop strategies and plans focused on fulfilling God's expectations for what we do and how we do it. As disciples, we must be obedient to God as revealed in His Word. As leaders, we must make sure our organizations and ministries are obedient to the whole counsel of Scripture, understanding that the Holy Spirit is involved in this process and that each ministry is part of a whole that we see dimly, but God sees clearly. Each ministry can have a different focus that majors on part of Scripture. For example, ministries may focus on feeding the poor or healing or education or evangelism or—you fill in the blank. But even when we fulfill part of Scripture, we have to be mindful of the whole counsel of Scripture and endeavor to fit into the big picture. We must not focus our piece of the picture without regard for the big picture.

If we are mindful of Kingdom metrics, we recognize that:

- Kingdom metrics are about Kingdom purposes (doing God's will).

- Kingdom metrics are about measuring our work by what God uses to measure us.

- Kingdom metrics are about obeying God's Word and teaching others to obey God's Word regardless of theological, doctrinal, denominational, church, or cultural bias.

- Kingdom metrics are about putting the Great Commandment and the Great Commission ahead of personal, denominational, church, or organizational objectives/goals.

- Kingdom metrics are transformational, which can only be accomplished by God working through all His people.

If we fail to include Kingdom metrics in our planning, we will fail to fulfill Kingdom purposes.

Following are some filter questions we use to determine if we are involved in Kingdom work instead of organizational work.

- Is the work founded on Scripture only, or is it doctrine-based?

- Is the work obedience-based, insight-based, or knowledge-based? (*Obedience-based* and *knowledge-based* are probably familiar terms. *Insight-based* is about discovering all the nuances of Scripture, but may not lead to obedience if insight is the goal. Most expositors and commentators are insight-based.)

- Does the work relate to the whole body of Christ?

- Does the work put the whole body of Christ ahead of our own personal or organizational interests?

- Does the work touch and benefit others not related to our organization?

- Does the work help others without expectation of return?

- Does the work take the Gospel to the masses (all demographics)?

- Does the work get to evangelism and church planting through disciple-making, and is disciple-making a primary focus?

- Even in its beginning stages, can others reproduce the work?

- Is the work founded on natural leaders?

- Do methodologies focus on multiplying new units—disciples, Discovery Groups, churches?

- Do methodologies focus on expanding to new neighborhoods, cities, nations, people groups?

- Do we plan to reach our city/nation/people group for Christ (focus on lostness), or do we want to grow our church/denomination (focus on ourselves)?

- Does the work put a high priority on reaching the lost regardless of other activities?

- Does the work endeavor to transform communities?

The Kingdom Parables give us some insight to Kingdom metrics (how God measures what we do):

- Sower and Soils (Matt. 13:1–23): The Gospel must be sowed in all soils, but only one of four soils produces fruit. Not everyone reacts the same way to the Word, but all are exposed to it.

- Wheat and Tares (Matt. 13:24–30, 36–43): Satan does his best to undermine the work of God. God does not ultimately deal with this until the end of the age.

- Mustard Seed and Leaven (Matt. 13:31–33): Kingdom work produces incredible growth and development.

- Hidden Treasure and Pearl of Great Price (Matt. 13:44–46): The Kingdom of God is worth everything we own. Some accidentally discover the Kingdom, while others actively search for it.

- Dragnet (Matt. 13:47–50): There will be judgment for the wicked and the righteous. Both the good news and the bad news need to be a part of our message. Our ministry must include both. We need to understand that evil will infiltrate what we do.

- Householder (Matt. 13:51–52): Those in the Kingdom of God treasure both the Old and the New Testaments, and are responsible to preserve, multiply, and teach both (the duty of scribes).

- Unmerciful Servant (Matt. 18:21–35): An unforgiving heart has no place in the Kingdom of God.

- Workers in the Vineyard (Matt. 18:1–16): All who respond to the Gospel gratefully, and work diligently during the time they have as a part of the Kingdom, receive the same reward—regardless of when they responded.

- Two Sons (Matt. 21:28–32): The Kingdom of God is filled with "doers," not "sayers." Obedience is our love response to God's mercy. (See Matthew 7:21–23; 28:20; John 14:15, 21, 23; 15:10, 14; 1 Corinthians 7:19; and 1 John 2:3–4.)

- Wicked Vinedressers (Matt. 21:33–46): The Kingdom of God will be taken from wicked religious leaders who reject

God's prophets, reject His Son, and do not bear fruit; and it will be given to those who accept the Son and bear fruit. (See Luke 12:48 for the responsibility of those who have been privileged to be a part of the Kingdom.)

- Wedding Banquet (Matt. 22:1–14): The Kingdom of God is for those who properly and thankfully receive the invitation of God (His grace) to join the feast.

- Ten Virgins (Matt. 25:1–13): The Kingdom of God is for those who are prepared for and watchful for the Lord's coming.

- Three Stewards (The Parable of the Talents) (Matt. 25:14–30): The Kingdom of God is for those who are found to be productive to the limits of their capacity when the Lord returns.

- Sheep and Goats (Matt. 25:13–46): The Kingdom of God is for those who unselfishly care for the poor and needy in society.

- Growing Seed (Mark 4:26–29): The Kingdom of God is made up of God and those who labor with Him; the increase comes from God, but we have to work.

- The other parables of Jesus also give us insight into Kingdom metrics. Luke 15 gives us three parables on lostness—the Lost Sheep, the Lost Coin, and the Lost Son (The Prodigal Son). In these parables, we see that God loves all His sheep, but His love is more than just collective love for His creation; it is individual love that looks for the lost and celebrates their return. Jesus died for the lost, and His love for the lost is our example.

Kingdom metrics come out of an understanding that God has plans and intentions for all we do, say, think, or fail to do in response to His Word. When we go about our personal lives or organizational lives without considering the Kingdom of God, we fail to be in step with God, and our work is hit-or-miss in regard to obeying God. Kingdom metrics ensure that we are trying to understand what our partnership with God looks like. We put what He wants first and then plan for our personal or organizational activities within the context of what God wants.

When we fail to start with Kingdom metrics, we risk missing what God wants us to do. We fail to be involved in what God has planned for His creation. We need to be asking ourselves the following questions:

- What does God expect from us?

- Does everything we are doing or planning fall within the context of God's plan?

- What do we need to change in order to be more Kingdom minded?

DEALING WITH DOUBT

The single biggest doubt we have when leading is, *Am I going the right way?* We have all spent time praying and planning, only to discover that the decision we made and/or the direction we took our followers was the wrong way or tangential to where we really wanted or needed to be. When we are blazing trails, there will be times when we go the wrong way, make mistakes, and even, sometimes, sin.

Two of our coworkers did something incredible a few summers ago. They and two other family members made the eight-thousand-plus-mile journey from Maine to Alaska in a forty-six-foot boat through the Northwest Passage. They were the first privately owned motor boat under sixty feet in length to ever make this passage unassisted by icebreakers. To put this in perspective, more people have climbed to the top of Mount Everest than have made it through the Northwest Passage in any kind of boat.

One of the events described by this intrepid team was their slog through pack ice. The lookout would direct the boat pilot, but sometimes they would hit a dead end. They would then try to retrace their route, but the sea currents and the wind had changed the configuration of the pack ice, and they would have to work their way to newly opened channels until they made it to open sea and were able to continue their planned route. The question in mind was always, "Are we going the right way?" At times their navigation equipment did not function properly because they were so close to the magnetic North Pole. They had no choice but to continue trying to find the right route to complete their journey. To quit was to die.

As leaders, we can't stop leading simply because we chose the wrong way or lose our way. We have to confess our sins and/ or mistakes, regroup the team, ask for input, determine the best direction to go with the information in hand, plan, retrain and resource the team, and start moving in the right direction. We depend on God through prayer and the Holy Spirit's guidance, but we don't stop leading; we don't stop listening; we don't stop moving.

Leadership requires us to push through personal failure, personal pain, personal biases, and the failures of our people. Leaders by influence have to have the patience to allow situations to mature, advise when goals are out of sync, and walk beside when necessary. What we do is about God's kingdom, not our personal empires. The results are eternal, not temporal. We will be judged by God, not other people.

So, if you are going to be a leader, then obedience, love, service, exemplary lives, courage, and adaptability are all part of the package. We also have to make tough decisions and understand that we will make mistakes. What separates great leaders from good leaders is

- an obedience to God;
- a striving toward excellence;
- humility in service;
- commitment to a vision;
- a determination to succeed;
- a willingness to risk;
- the ability to forgive;
- courage to change;
- a desire to learn;
- the ability to recruit teams to our weaknesses;
- a capacity to strategize and implement plans;
- the ability to make more leaders; and
- the determination to never quit.

MENTORING

A few years ago, Cityteam had a partnership with an organization in a limited-access country. This organization wanted to see a Disciple-Making Movement sweep through their country, but they didn't know how to get things started.

They sent several leaders to our trainings. One leader in particular really leaned into the concepts and applied them throughout his existing networks. He began to see Discovery Groups started in villages throughout the area. These groups multiplied several times. Everyone was excited, and this leader became a rising star for disciple-making and church planting in the area.

Then we began to hear some things that disturbed us. One young woman came forward saying the young leader was acting inappropriately toward her. We immediately investigated. Unfortunately, the investigation revealed that the leader had been using his position to take advantage of young women in multiple groups. We disciplined the young leader, but his groups never recovered from his betrayal. Church planting was set back in that area for quite some time.

We thought a long time about what went wrong. We gave the young man all the knowledge he needed to be a successful disciple-maker. And for a time, he was very successful. Knowledge transfer, however, is not disciple-making. We failed to disciple the leader in every area of his life. Consequently, we didn't pick up on what were initially small character flaws that eventually became ministry-ending, life-shattering problems. We failed to mentor, and the consequences were disastrous.

MAKING DISCIPLE-MAKERS

In the modern church, discipleship is an educational process designed to orient new believers to the biblical and historical practices of our churches. Even in some extremely Bible-oriented materials, the emphasis is on knowing God's Word, with some admonition to obey, but without the relationship necessary to see if it happens. There is a misconception that if people know what is right, they will do what is right. Experience tells us that this is not the case, yet we function as if it is.

The root of discipleship is a relationship with Jesus that transforms our hearts, minds, and behaviors to be what Jesus teaches and demands they should be. Through the disciples' relationships with one another—especially between mature believers and new believers—there is personal and collective growth. Disciple-making relationships positively impact all walks of life and all relationships in family, community, business, and government.

Transmitting information in the discipleship process is imperative, but it is not the most important aspect of the disciple-making process. Disciples do not just know what the Master requires; they do what the Master requires in every situation regardless of the consequences. Not every situation is delineated in Scripture, but all the principles are there for disciples to apply to daily living. Understanding the principles of Scripture and knowing the mind of God are crucial in the disciple-making process.

Where new believers or not-yet-believers are concerned, principles are difficult to see and apply to the many situations in which they find themselves. They need the influence of mature disciples in their lives, and they need relationships with these mature disciples that permit them to discuss any aspect of life, deal with any problems or sins they may have, and grow through experience as wisdom replaces knowledge. (Wisdom is using what you know to do what is right. Wisdom requires knowledge, but knowledge does not imply wisdom.)

Mentoring is the intentional relationship with others that causes all parties involved to grow in discipleship, the process of converting knowledge to wisdom. Mentors help new believers learn Scripture and walk the narrow path demanded by Scripture. Maturing believers need to be mentors to grow in their own discipleship.

A church without discipleship is doomed. Not-yet-believers and new believers have no examples to follow and no mature believers assisting them in their discipleship. Mature believers do not have people to pour their lives into, and as a result, stop growing or fail to grow.

The disciple-making mentoring relationship is a win-win situation for all involved. Pre-believers and new believers have examples of maturity in their lives to invest in them and hold them accountable. Mature believers have people in their lives who ask the hard questions and challenge the status quo, thus driving them to learn and perfect their lives.

The moment these relationships do not exist in our churches, we find ourselves in a lose-lose situation. Not-yet-believers and new believers have no examples to follow, no one to provide wise counsel, and no accountability. Mature believers have no one to spur them on to new levels of knowledge and new levels of wisdom as knowledge turns to actions in thought and deed. They also have no observers to challenge them to live better lives, or to hold them accountable by being present, making observations, and asking questions.

All believers should simultaneously be mentoring others while also being mentored themselves. As disciple-makers mature, they discover their mentoring relationships become peer relationships that allow them to learn from one another and spur one another to new heights of obedience and success.

In the mentoring/disciple-making relationship, no area of life is off-limits, including relationships to God, family, community and church, call and work, and even to ourselves as we develop mentally, spiritually, emotionally and physically. We need to engage in a question-and-answer process that reveals the disciple-maker's thoughts and actions. There should be enough personal contact to verify the life of a disciple and the life of the disciple-maker. Words are good, but seeing words put into action are foundational for the mentoring/disciple-making process. If a disciple-maker is never in the new disciple's home, or never sees the new disciple outside of a knowledge acquisition environment, then there is no mentoring/disciple-making relationship. There is only a teacher/student relationship, which facilitates knowledge flow but not disciple-making.

Mentoring and disciple-making are one and the same. They require relationship and accountability on top of knowledge building. They cause knowledge to become wisdom, which is making the right choices and doing the right things because of your knowledge and experience. As Scripture says:

> Do not merely listen to the word, and so deceive yourselves. Do what it says. Anyone who listens to the word but does not do what it says is like a man who looks at his face in a mirror and, after looking at himself, goes away

and immediately forgets what he looks like. But the man who looks intently into the perfect law that gives freedom, and continues to do this, not forgetting what he has heard, but doing it—he will be blessed in what he does. (James 1:22–25)

I am not writing this to shame you, but to warn you, as my dear children. Even though you have ten thousand guardians in Christ, you do not have many fathers, for in Christ Jesus I became your father through the gospel. Therefore I urge you to imitate me. For this reason I am sending to you Timothy, my son whom I love, who is faithful in the Lord. He will remind you of my way of life in Christ Jesus, which agrees with what I teach everywhere in every church. (1 Cor. 4:14–17)

For we know, brothers loved by God, that he has chosen you, because our gospel came to you not simply with words, but also with power, with the Holy Spirit and with deep conviction. You know how we lived among you for your sake. You became imitators of us and of the Lord; in spite of severe suffering, you welcomed the message with the joy given by the Holy Spirit. And so you became a model to all the believers in Macedonia and Achaia. The Lord's message rang out from you not only in Macedonia and Achaia—your faith in God has become known everywhere. Therefore we do not need to say anything about it, for they themselves report what kind of reception you gave us. They tell how you turned to God from idols to serve the living and true God, and to wait for his Son from heaven, whom he raised from the dead—Jesus, who rescues us from the coming wrath. (1 Thess. 1:4–10)

Remember your leaders, who spoke the word of God to you. Consider the outcome of their way of life and imitate their faith. Jesus Christ is the same yesterday and today and forever. (Heb. 13:7–8)

The desired outcome of mentoring and disciple-making is well-rounded men and women of God who can make disciples and coach others to make disciples, start churches and coach others to start churches, and lead Disciple-Making Movements and coach others to lead Disciple-Making Movements. But as we said before, disciple-making is more than a job; it is a lifestyle. One doesn't "do" disciple-making; he or she lives the life of a disciple-maker—which requires us to be mentors, and mentoring begins with oneself.

The single greatest indictment of religious leaders is found in Matthew 23:

> "The teachers of the law and the Pharisees sit in Moses' seat. So you must obey them and do everything they tell you. But do not do what they do, for they do not practice what they preach. They tie up heavy loads and put them on men's shoulders, but they themselves are not willing to lift a finger to move them.
>
> "Everything they do is done for men to see: They make their phylacteries wide and the tassels on their garments long; they love the place of honor at banquets and the most important seats in the synagogues; they love to be greeted in the marketplaces and to have men call them 'Rabbi.'
>
> "But you are not to be called 'Rabbi,' for you have only one Master and you are all brothers. And do not call anyone on earth 'father,' for you have one Father, and he is in heaven. Nor are you to be called 'teacher,' for you have one Teacher, the Christ. The greatest among you will be your servant. For whoever exalts himself will be humbled, and whoever humbles himself will be exalted.

"Woe to you, teachers of the law and Pharisees, you hypocrites! You shut the kingdom of heaven in men's faces. You yourselves do not enter, nor will you let those enter who are trying to.

"Woe to you, teachers of the law and Pharisees, you hypocrites! You travel over land and sea to win a single convert, and when he becomes one, you make him twice as much a son of hell as you are.

"Woe to you, blind guides! You say, 'If anyone swears by the temple, it means nothing; but if anyone swears by the gold of the temple, he is bound by his oath.' You blind fools! Which is greater: the gold, or the temple that makes the gold sacred? You also say, 'If anyone swears by the altar, it means nothing; but if anyone swears by the gift on it, he is bound by his oath.' You blind men! Which is greater: the gift, or the altar that makes the gift sacred? Therefore, he who swears by the altar swears by it and by everything on it. And he who swears by the temple swears by it and by the one who dwells in it. And he who swears by heaven swears by God's throne and by the one who sits on it.

"Woe to you, teachers of the law and Pharisees, you hypocrites! You give a tenth of your spices—mint, dill and cummin. But you have neglected the more important matters of the law—justice, mercy and faithfulness. You should have practiced the latter, without neglecting the former. You blind guides! You strain out a gnat but swallow a camel.

"Woe to you, teachers of the law and Pharisees, you hypocrites! You clean the outside of the cup and dish, but inside they are full of greed and self-indulgence. Blind Pharisee! First clean the inside of the cup and dish, and then the outside also will be clean.

"Woe to you, teachers of the law and Pharisees, you hypocrites! You are like whitewashed tombs, which look beautiful on the outside but on the inside are full of dead men's bones and everything unclean. In the same way, on the outside you appear to people as righteous but on the inside you are full of hypocrisy and wickedness.

"Woe to you, teachers of the law and Pharisees, you hypocrites! You build tombs for the prophets and decorate the graves of the righteous. And you say, 'If we had lived in the days of our forefathers, we would not have taken part with them in shedding the blood of the prophets.' So you testify against yourselves that you are the descendants of those who murdered the prophets. Fill up, then, the measure of the sin of your forefathers!

"You snakes! You brood of vipers! How will you escape being condemned to hell? Therefore I am sending you prophets and wise men and teachers. Some of them you will kill and crucify; others you will flog in your synagogues and pursue from town to town. And so upon you will come all the righteous blood that has been shed on earth, from the blood of righteous Abel to the blood of Zechariah son of Berekiah, whom you murdered between the temple and the altar. I tell you the truth, all this will come upon this generation.

"O Jerusalem, Jerusalem, you who kill the prophets and stone those sent to you, how often I have longed to gather your children together, as a hen gathers her chicks under her wings, but you were not willing. Look, your house is left to you desolate. For I tell you, you will not see me again until you say, 'Blessed is he who comes in the name of the Lord.'"

There is a lot in this passage, but the main point is that the religious leaders did not live out what they taught. Their public and private lives were not consistent with the demands of Scripture.

- They did not practice what they preached.

- They put burdens on people instead of helping them with their burdens.

- They did what they did for themselves instead of for God.

- They shut the Kingdom of God instead of opening it.

- They made converts who were worse than they were.

- They forgot the source of their oaths.

- They were rule makers and rule police, but forgot the teachings of the law regarding justice, mercy, and righteousness.

- They looked good on the outside, but inside were dirty and corrupt. (The whitewashed graves looked nice, but were meant to warn pilgrims not to inadvertently touch them and be disqualified by the law from entering the Temple at Passover. If you touched a tomb you disqualified yourself from worship.)

- They were so dangerous to the people around them that they were like a brood of vipers—certain death if touched.

These warnings apply also to those of us who lead. Falling into the sin of the Pharisees is so easy. Our positions, our leadership, our rules, our representing God to the lost and leading the saved can cause us to lose sight of being a servant of God— one who humbles himself or herself and whom God exalts as we serve His creation.

True mentoring begins in the heart of the mentor. Mentoring is not just what we know; our experiences and what we learned from them make us mentors. Mentoring is also what we avoid, what we choose not to do, as well as how we choose to relate to God and other people in public and in private.

Mentors strive for consistency in their lives. Their deepest desire is to know God and serve His people. They are even-keeled. What you see in public is what you get in private. And the life of a "sinner who has been redeemed by the blood of Christ and raised up to walk a new life" is not a slogan, but a revealed lived-in and lived-out reality that permeates all that mentors think, do, and say.

Mentors are redeemed sinners who know it every day, and live out the sainthood that has been bestowed on them by Christ for the benefit of the Kingdom of God and the people they serve. If God is not working on those of us who call ourselves mentors, then we have no basis on which to be a mentor. Mentoring is not about being perfect; it's about striving for perfection through the mercy and grace of God. Mentoring is not about knowing everything; it's about being a learner who shares hard-earned lessons with others in hopes that the lessons can be a little less hard. Mentoring is not about being long-term (old) in a field of endeavor; it's about being wise and able to apply the lessons learned to everyday life for the benefit of others more than self.

If you want to be a mentor, you have to start with self. As you learn, fail, repent, and repeat, you bring others along with you. Your life is intertwined with the lives of others—from family to old friends to new friends, and even to enemies. Each relationship has a potential for happiness or bitterness. Each moment is an opportunity to choose to do right, do wrong, or do nothing (which may be the best or worst decision of all). Each task can succeed or fail, sometimes regardless of what we are doing.

Mentoring is sharing your life with others so that you and they will be better people in service to the Kingdom of God.

The call to be a mentor demands your best in all situations and relationships for the good of others involved in Kingdom work.

MENTORING VALUES

Core values are our default position for everything we think and do. Core values are best discovered in those situations in which we find ourselves under extreme stress. We all want to be cut some slack when we are under stress, and we need to cut each other slack at these times. Extreme stress doesn't usually bring out our best. But when we are under extreme stress we think and respond at our core value levels. You see, core values are not a list of nice thoughts and desired behaviors we put on paper. They are the default position from which we make decisions and take actions without the need for excessive thought. Therefore, when we are under stress and have minimal time or energy to think, our core values come out in what we think, say, or do, as well as what we choose not to think, not to say, or not to do.

I (David) remember my early days as a Christian. My youth director was my mentor, and he worked with me on my language (specifically, cursing). I felt successful when I stopped using curse words, but my mentor asked me about what I thought, not just what I said. I still needed to work on my thoughts. I remember the day when an event that would have usually resulted in a long litany of cursing actually ended without even a thought of a curse. Wow! I knew then I had changed. My core values had adjusted. I kept working. Then I remember the day when a very stressful event occurred and my thoughts were of what was best for the other person, not about me. I felt I had taken a step into a place that was more like Christ.

Please understand, I'm not saying I'm perfect. I still slip and slide. But I intentionally strive to be more like Christ every day in what I think, say, and do. These are the core values of a Christian. Paul put it this way:

> But whatever was to my profit I now consider loss for the sake of Christ. What is more, I consider everything a loss compared to the surpassing greatness of knowing Christ Jesus my Lord, for whose sake I have lost all things. I consider them rubbish, that I may gain Christ and be found in him, not having a righteousness of my own that comes from the law, but that which is through faith in Christ—the righteousness that comes from God and is by faith. I want to know Christ and the power of his resurrection and the fellowship of sharing in his sufferings, becoming like him in his death, and so, somehow, to attain to the resurrection from the dead.
>
> Not that I have already obtained all this, or have already been made perfect, but I press on to take hold of that for which Christ Jesus took hold of me. Brothers, I do not consider myself yet to have taken hold of it. But one thing I do: Forgetting what is behind and straining toward what is ahead, I press on toward the goal to win the prize for which God has called me heavenward in Christ Jesus. All of us who are mature should take such a view of things. And if on some point you think differently, that too God will make clear to you. Only let us live up to what we have already attained. (Phil 3:7–16)

Mentors help mentees adjust their core values to be more like Christ in every area of their lives. The focus is not on the job but on the person.

If we focus on the job, we are coaches, not mentors. Now, there are times when mentors have to coach, but our focus is not the job; it's the person.

If we focus on knowledge, we are teachers, not mentors. There are times when mentors have to teach, but our focus is not gaining or giving knowledge; it's the person.

Mentors focus on every aspect of a person's life. To impact everything in someone's life requires us to help her adjust her core values to a biblical perspective.

Look at what Paul said to the Ephesians:

So I tell you this, and insist on it in the Lord, that you must no longer live as the Gentiles do, in the futility of their thinking. They are darkened in their understanding and separated from the life of God because of the ignorance that is in them due to the hardening of their hearts. Having lost all sensitivity, they have given themselves over to sensuality so as to indulge in every kind of impurity, with a continual lust for more.

You, however, did not come to know Christ that way. Surely you heard of him and were taught in him in accordance with the truth that is in Jesus. You were taught, with regard to your former way of life, to put off your old self, which is being corrupted by its deceitful desires; to be made new in the attitude of your minds; and to put on the new self, created to be like God in true righteousness and holiness.

Therefore each of you must put off falsehood and speak truthfully to his neighbor, for we are all members of one body. "In your anger do not sin": Do not let the sun go down while you are still angry, and do not give the devil a foothold. He who has been stealing must steal no longer, but must work, doing something useful with his own hands, that he may have something to share with those in need.

Do not let any unwholesome talk come out of your mouths, but only what is helpful for building others up according to their needs, that it may benefit those who listen. And do not grieve the Holy Spirit of God, with whom you were sealed for the day of redemption. Get rid of all bitterness, rage and anger, brawling and slander, along with every form of malice. Be kind and compassionate to one another, forgiving each other, just as in Christ God forgave you.

Be imitators of God, therefore, as dearly loved children and live a life of love, just as Christ loved us and gave himself up for us as a fragrant offering and sacrifice to God.

But among you there must not be even a hint of sexual immorality, or of any kind of impurity, or of greed, because these are improper for God's holy people. Nor should there be obscenity, foolish talk or coarse joking, which are out of place, but rather thanksgiving. For of this you can be sure: No immoral, impure or greedy person—such a man is an idolater—has any inheritance in the kingdom of Christ and of God. Let no one deceive you with empty words, for because of such things God's wrath comes on those who are disobedient. Therefore do not be partners with them.

For you were once darkness, but now you are light in the Lord. Live as children of light (for the fruit of the light consists in all goodness, righteousness and truth) and find out what pleases the Lord. Have nothing to do with the fruitless deeds of darkness, but rather expose them. For it is shameful even to mention what the disobedient do in secret. But everything exposed by the light becomes visible, for it is light that makes everything visible. This is why it is said: "Wake up, O sleeper, rise from the dead, and Christ will shine on you."

Be very careful, then, how you live—not as unwise but as wise, making the most of every opportunity, because the days are evil. Therefore do not be foolish, but understand what the Lord's will is. Do not get drunk on wine, which leads to debauchery. Instead, be filled with the Spirit. Speak to one another with psalms, hymns and spiritual songs. Sing and make music in your heart to the Lord, always giving thanks to God the Father for everything, in the name of our Lord Jesus Christ. (Eph. 4:17—5:20)

Mentors help mentees become more like Christ in all they do. This includes the following:

1. Their relationship to God;

2. Their relationship to family and friends;

3. Their relationship to the community at large and the church;

4. Their fulfillment of God's call in their lives;

5. Their vocations (how they put food on the table);

6. Their relationship to themselves (including general knowledge, work skills, mental health, emotional health, spiritual health, and physical health).

This level of mentorship cannot be achieved with meetings or seminars. Mentoring requires investing in each other's lives in such a way that we are pressed by the Holy Spirit from all directions to become more like Christ—adjusting our core values to those revealed in the Word of God.

HELPING MENTEES BECOME PEERS

Mentoring is a two-way relationship in which both participants learn and grow. Great mentors are learners, and there is no greater learning opportunity than to guide others in their discoveries, and discover afresh what we have known and forgotten, and to delight in finding out new things through and with our mentees.

Change characterizes the mentoring relationship. The goal of mentoring is the development of the mentee into a disciplemaker, a leader maker. Achieving our goal requires continuous learning, growth and change. The very act of mentoring changes and matures the mentor as well as the mentee. This is the reason it's so important to encourage mentees to mentor others. Unless and until they mentor others, the mentoring process is of limited value.

We have a very firm rule for those we mentor—mentees must actively mentor others or we will not spend time mentoring them. One of Satan's primary attacks on Christianity is to get leaders to mentor people who simply absorb their time and efforts and give little return. They do not pass on what they learn, and thus fail to grow. Mentors must be wise as serpents—in other words, see where Satan is going to attack and avoid those situations. Getting Christian leaders to use their time in non-reproducing relationships is a tremendous loss for Kingdom work.

Mentoring relationships mature over time. A lot of teaching and training go into the mentoring process, at least at first. As the mentee learns lessons and practices skills, he or she teaches and trains others. (Knowledge and skill sets are not learned until one teaches and trains others.) Guiding others increases capacity for leadership. Leaders cannot mature without making new leaders. Making new leaders helps mentors learn more about themselves. Mentors learn more about leading as we observe and assist our mentees in their leadership development.

If the mentoring relationship works, in a relatively short time the relationship moves from one of mentor and mentee to coworker and peer. This has been known to happen in as little as one year, but more often it takes three to five years. If a mentor gets stuck in a mentor-mentee relationship for more than five years, there is a serious problem. Most often, this is because the mentee is not reproducing. And this happens when the mentor makes a student instead of a leader.

Leaders make more leaders. As a leader makes more leaders, he or she matures quickly. Developing people is an excellent way to grow. The more people we mentor, the more we are exposed to new ideas, new problems to solve, new opportunities to learn, new relationships, and new successes and failures from which to learn.

When the mentoring process is right, the relationship transitions from mentor to peer very quickly. If a mentor misses this transition regularly, then he must evaluate his mentoring relationships. Mentors should ask the following questions when evaluating their mentoring relationships.

- Is there an agreement in place that outlines the mentoring relationship? (This doesn't have to be a formal written document, but should be mutually understood.)

- Are my mentees and I covering all the areas of life that make great leaders? (Relationship to God, family, community, and church—including peers and others, our call from God, our jobs—how we financially support our families and selves, and our mental, emotional, spiritual, and physical health.)

- Is my mentee mentoring others? (A mentor should meet the mentees of his or her mentee.)

◉ What am I learning from my mentee, including successes and failures? (If a mentor doesn't learn from his or her mentees, something is wrong.)

◉ Is there success in both of our lives as a result of the mentoring relationship? (Are the mentor and mentee better people because of their relationship?)

◉ Is the relationship growing and changing?

◉ What could, or should, we do better to improve the relationship and its outcomes?

◉ Have I made students or leaders? (Teaching and coaching are so much easier than mentoring. Focusing on the information or skill set without concern for how it's used in leadership development is an easy trap. In true mentoring, mentors must know how the information or skill sets are passed along as mentees make more leaders. The mentor-mentee relationship requires accountability.)

Seeing mentees become peers is incredibly rewarding. This does not happen by accident. Mentors must be intentional in the relationship, and brutal in evaluating their performance as mentors.

MENTORING THROUGH CONFLICT

Humor in Western media is built on conflict and the mismanagement of conflict. A generation of leaders grew up watching television and cinema personalities use sarcasm, pithy comebacks, personal attack (emotional and/or physical), and clandestinely getting even as a cultural norm for dealing with conflicts involving family, friends, coworkers, and strangers. This may be humorous on the screen, but the results in real life are disastrous and range from strained relationships to devastated relationships to broken relationships to revenge (the intentional harming of another because of perceived or real harm from him/her).

Conflict is a normal part of human interaction. It's going to happen! Everyone makes mistakes that impact others. People choose to misbehave or sin in ways that hurt others emotionally and/or physically. How mentors respond to conflict or events that may lead to conflict defines who they are. How mentors respond to conflict determines if we grow as leaders or not. In fact, dealing with conflict appropriately is a prerequisite for deepening and maturing relationships and growing as a leader. Inappropriately dealing with conflict causes loss of trust and a pulling away from the relationship. Appropriately dealing with conflict builds trust and leads to deeper, more meaningful relationships.

Inappropriate ways of dealing with conflict or problems include the following:

- Ignoring the problem. Problems won't go away; ignoring them makes things worse.

- Disrespecting the other person. Disrespect begets disrespect, closes down communication, destroys existing trust, and builds mistrust.

- Complaining. However, venting is not the same as complaining. Venting is a necessary verbal process that allows one to put things in perspective and in order. Venting should be done in private with a trusted person who will keep information confidential and will make sure the beneficial venting does not turn into destructive complaining. I don't generally vent to my wife because it may cause her to dislike or have reservations about the person on the other side of the problem. If the other side is a friend or a colleague, you can understand why this can be a problem. I cause her to have negative feelings about the person based on my venting, not on a rational evaluation of the problem in the context of the whole relationship.

- Delaying dealing with the problem. Problems only get bigger.

- Being indirect in reaction, action, and communication. This leads to misunderstanding, drags others into the problem, and slows resolution of problems, if they are solved at all.

- Retaliating! This starts feuds.

- Shouting loud enough so that sensible people go away and avoid the confrontation.

- Resorting to personal attacks instead of dealing with the issue(s) at hand.

- Anything physical, including rude gestures.

- Being critical.

- Making the point as forcefully as possible.

- Thinking of a good comeback for the last statement.

- Ignoring it if you don't like it.

- Talking to avoid listening.

- Building support among friends and peers for one side of the argument.

- Dragging others into the argument.

- Not letting others have their say or share their side of the issue.

- Assigning motives for another's behavior. It is not possible to know another person's motives until and unless he or she shares them. Even when there is a history of bad behavior or bad decisions, mentors must never assume they know the motives behind the behavior or decision.

- Sarcasm of any kind.

- Dealing with a problem during the heat of emotion. High emotion causes high emotion, which stops listening and causes bad decisions and bad behavior.

- Dragging past experiences into the argument instead of dealing with the current issue. This is less likely to happen if mentors dealt with previous issues appropriately.

- Using superlatives like "always" and "never."

- Using threatening or defensive body language.

- Using insulting, abusive, and/or profane language.

- Taking the fight public. Having a third party present during serious discussions is different from taking the fight public.

- Using email, instant messaging, or text messaging to address any problem. In person is best, but video or audio conferencing is acceptable if a face-to-face meeting is not possible.

Sometimes people react confrontationally, aggressively, and openly (name-calling, embarrassing another, arguments, shouting matches, nose-to-nose stare downs, gathering allies, and even physical violence). Sometimes people take action passively (defensiveness; avoiding contact; snide, mean, or cutting remarks; sarcasm; spreading rumors; gossip; backstabbing or backbiting; attacks on another's integrity; sabotaging projects; or causing physical, economic, or emotional harm indirectly in a way that cannot be traced back to us).

A common phrase is, "He threw me under the bus!" This statement is terrible for a number of reasons:

- It's violent.

- It assigns negative motives of intentional harm to another.

- It suggests little possibility of recovery from the event.

- It is almost always followed by a declaration of how to throw the other person under the bus.

Anger, embarrassment, frustration, and disappointment are all honest emotions. But we must understand that we may be mistaken about what caused the emotion. And even when we have a legitimate reason for our emotions, we can choose how we deal with them. Dealing with these emotions appropriately is the first step to a fair fight. When we deal with these emotions inappropriately through ineffective communication (which includes not dealing with our emotions), we elevate the emotion to a point of willingness to fight or cause harm to another directly or indirectly. Our emotional energy has to go somewhere. The more we don't appropriately deal with our emotion(s) and the situation that is causing the emotion(s), the more likely our emotional energy will erupt in an inappropriate and untimely manner, causing harm to relationships and resulting in conflict that will be more difficult or impossible to resolve.

Here are some ways to deal with emotion appropriately:

- Own the emotion. Identify and accept that you are angry, embarrassed, frustrated, or disappointed. I (David) am a thinker, not a feeler. When something gets bad enough or good enough to force emotions from me, I have to spend a lot of time sorting out the feelings and work on how to communicate what I am feeling. This takes time. I (Paul) am a feeler. Feelers tend to dump their emotion on others quickly, without analyzing what caused the emotion and why they are feeling the way they are, or what the results of the dump will be. Feelers need to process before spilling their guts, or they will exacerbate problems. Both feelers and thinkers need discipline when dealing with emotions and difficult situations.

- Ask help-me-to-understand questions, and don't assume or assign motives. I (David) was on the freeway one night, and the car behind me was following with its high beams on. When I slowed down to let the car pass, it would slow down and stay behind me. Soon there was a fuel stop, and I exited to get away from this guy, but he followed me to the fuel stop. With a little fear and a lot of anger I jumped out of my car ready for a fight, but decided to ask if there were a problem as politely as I could. A little old lady got out of the car and exclaimed, "I'm so sorry about my headlights! They're stuck on high, and I was looking for the next place to get help." We must not assume we understand why people are acting in a way that irritates, frustrates, or angers us.

◉ Discuss the problem with a trusted ally who will help you through the issues and keep your confidence. With serious problems this may mean a professional counselor who is impartial and will help you deal with your stuff before you try to deal with the problem.

◉ State your problem, and then give the other person time to deal with her emotions before you continue. You may have to ask, "Do you need time to process this?" If she is demonstrating high emotion or is trying to hide her emotions, you may need to say, "I want to give you time to process this. Let's meet and talk in an hour or so." High emotion exacerbates the situation and makes it hard to hear the other person. It causes us to think and say things we regret. High emotion is a component of fighting and is not good for problem solving. Cool heads solve problems. Hot heads cause problems.

◉ Give meaningful feedback regarding emotions. Don't assume you understand or are being understood. Use sentences like "I'm frustrated because . . ." or "I'm angry about . . ." Be reflective in regard to another's emotions. Use sentences like "I understand you are angry about . . ." or "Can you help me understand your frustration regarding . . . ?"

Another problem in many disagreements (fights) is the well-meaning third party who wants to defend one of the participants in the disagreement or who simply jumps in to defend a friend or teammate. Fighting for or defending others impairs their development in leadership. Don't do it and don't allow it. When there is disagreement, only the parties involved should be addressing the situation unless it has degenerated to a point that no one is listening, and then an impartial mediator may be appropriate. People who are not a part of the problem and who infuse themselves into defending or trying to solve the problem on another's behalf actually compound the problem. Now there are three instead of two involved in the problem. The person who isn't represented becomes more frustrated, and the one who is being defended takes a passive role, which stunts his or her leadership development. Leaders must learn how to deal with problems on their own. They can seek advice, but they must deal with the problem themselves. Defending or representing a person in a fight takes away his opportunity to grow, even if the fight isn't fair. Third parties can debrief the fight, but should never participate in a fight. Debriefing is a learning activity. Participating causes more problems.

Leaders must understand that mistakes are always in the past. Solutions are developed and are always in the future. We cannot change the past, but we can influence the future by the decisions we make. Accountability and problem solving are about the future, not the past. When there is a problem, we must seek solution, even when the problem is repetitive bad behavior or poor decision making. Try to state the problem as simply and directly as possible. The fewer words used to characterize the problem, the likelier we are to quickly and efficiently solve the problem.

Find ways for both sides of the problem to feel valued and have a voice in the problem-solving discussion. We must watch ourselves to determine if we are unresponsive and/ or uninterested in the other's perspective. This can manifest itself when we do more talking than listening. Other ineffective ways of communicating include being dishonest, hostile, or critical. Avoid controlling or manipulating another while communicating. Remember, the goal of communication is to make our thoughts and feelings known and understood. We cannot control the other person's response or actions. We need to remember that attempting to be right and to win the argument is ineffective. It may be tempting to try to "win," but the relationship will lose.

Good communication is honest, open, and direct. It leaves no doubt as to the purpose and the meaning of our words. We have to overcome our cultural bias and fear of stating our true thoughts and feelings. This should be done in a gracious and respectful way. Allow the other person to speak and respond while we listen. Listen to what the other person is saying, and try to understand and interpret it correctly. Ask questions for information and clarity when you don't understand or you doubt what is being said. Good communication requires us to make sure others understand us and that we understand them. Good communication leads to trust, which is a primary ingredient for problem solving.

The Bible has a lot to say about avoiding problems and dealing with problems. Take a look at the following Scripture passages. As you read through them, ask God to show you how to apply them to your current problems with other people.

Accept one another, then, just as Christ accepted you, in order to bring praise to God. (Rom. 15:7)

I appeal to you, brothers, in the name of our Lord Jesus Christ, that all of you agree with one another so that there may be no divisions among you and that you may be perfectly united in mind and thought. (1 Cor. 1:10)

Bear with each other and forgive whatever grievances you may have against one another. Forgive as the Lord forgave you. (Col. 3:13)

Do nothing out of selfish ambition or vain conceit, but in humility consider others better than yourselves. (Phil. 2:3)

Do not let any unwholesome talk come out of your mouths, but only what is helpful for building others up according to their needs, that it may benefit those who listen. (Eph. 4:29)

Carry each other's burdens, and in this way you will fulfill the law of Christ. (Gal. 6:2)

Each one should test his own actions. Then he can take pride in himself, without comparing himself to somebody else, for each one should carry his own load. (Gal. 6:4–5)

There should be no division in the body, but that its parts should have equal concern for each other. If one part suffers, every part suffers with it; if one part is honored, every part rejoices with it. Now you are the body of Christ, and each one of you is a part of it. (1 Cor. 12:25–27)

Therefore confess your sins to each other and pray for each other so that you may be healed. The prayer of a righteous man is powerful and effective. (James 5:16)

If you keep on biting and devouring each other, watch out or you will be destroyed by each other. (Gal. 5:15)

Be devoted to one another in brotherly love. Honor one another above yourselves. (Rom. 12:10)

They said to one another, "Surely we are being punished because of our brother. We saw how distressed he was when he pleaded with us for his life, but we would not listen; that's why this distress has come upon us." (Gen. 42:21)

Therefore encourage one another and build each other up, just as in fact you are doing. (1 Thess. 5:11)

But encourage one another daily, as long as it is called Today, so that none of you may be hardened by sin's deceitfulness. (Heb. 3:13)

And let us consider how we may spur one another on toward love and good deeds. (Heb. 10:24)

Then Peter came to Jesus and asked, "Lord, how many times shall I forgive my brother when he sins against me? Up to seven times? Jesus answered, "I tell you, not seven times, but seventy-seven times.

"Therefore, the kingdom of heaven is like a king who wanted to settle accounts with his servants. As he began the settlement, a man who owed him ten thousand talents was brought to him. Since he was not able to pay, the master ordered that he and his wife and his children and all that he had be sold to repay the debt.

"The servant fell on his knees before him. 'Be patient with me,' he begged, 'and I will pay back everything.' The servant's master took pity on him, canceled the debt and let him go.

"But when that servant went out, he found one of his fellow servants who owed him a hundred denarii. He grabbed him and began to choke him. 'Pay back what you owe me!' he demanded.

"His fellow servant fell to his knees and begged him, 'Be patient with me, and I will pay you back.'

"But he refused. Instead, he went off and had the man thrown into prison until he could pay the debt. When the other servants saw what had happened, they were greatly distressed and went and told their master everything that had happened.

"Then the master called the servant in. "You wicked servant,' he said, 'I canceled all that debt of yours because you begged me to. Shouldn't you have had mercy on your fellow servant just as I had on you?' In anger his master turned him over to the jailers to be tortured, until he should pay back all he owed.

"This is how my heavenly Father will treat each of you unless you forgive your brother from your heart." (Matt. 18:21–35)

Don't grumble against each other, brothers, or you will be judged. The Judge is standing at the door!" (James 5:9)

Live in harmony with one another. Do not be proud, but be willing to associate with people of low position. Do not be conceited. (Rom. 12:16)

Finally, all of you, live in harmony with one another; be sympathetic, love as brothers, be compassionate and humble. (1 Peter 3:8)

A few years ago, Cityteam's leadership team noticed an alarming trend in some of the Disciple-Making Movements in Africa—they were plateauing. In some cases, even declining. Immediately, we started looking for answers.

We discovered that we had done a really good job training high-capacity leaders. And in turn, these leaders had trained others. But as we've said before, training is only about knowledge and skill transfer, not capacity building or character building. Consequently, each of these leaders saw incredible results as they were equipped with more effective tools. But when those results pushed them to the limits of their capacity as leaders, they hit a major roadblock.

We had to move past training leaders and move into mentoring leaders. Furthermore, we had to help these leaders learn how to mentor other leaders. Our hypothesis was that we would see a lift in disciple-making and church planting across the entire network.

Sure enough, we saw disciple-making and church planting increase. We realized that mere knowledge transfer wasn't enough to sustain a movement. If you want to sustain a movement, you must invest in increasing the capacity of leaders. If you want to sustain a Disciple-Making Movement, you must mentor.

AFTERWORD

A couple of years ago I (David) sat down with a church planter in India. "I am a millionaire," the church planter said.

"What do you mean?"

He grinned. "This year we baptized the one millionth Bhojpuri into the Kingdom. In God's economy, that makes me a millionaire."

I couldn't stop the tears. At the time of this conversation, just twelve years into our ministry among the Bhojpuri, we had baptized over a million new brothers and sisters into the Kingdom of heaven and started more than forty thousand churches.

I had no idea that people would look back on what God did with my failure and call it a "movement."

I never dreamed He would make me a millionaire.

We pray, with all our hearts, that you become millionaires as well and that all of heaven will rejoice over lost people who will fall in love with Jesus because you became a disciple-maker focused on reaching the lost sheep who will never come to our churches.

APPENDIX

LIST OF STUDIES FOR NON-CHRISTIANS

SCRIPTURE PASSAGE	STORY
Genesis 1:1–25	The Creation Story: God Created the World
Genesis 2:4–24	The Creation Story: The Creation of Man
Genesis 3:1–13	The Fall: The First Sin and Judgment
Genesis 3:14–24	The Fall: Judgment of a Sinful World
Genesis 6:1–9:17	The Fall: The Flood
Genesis 12:1–8; 15:1–6	Redemption: God's Promise to Abram
Genesis 22:1–19	Redemption: Abraham offers Isaac as a Sacrifice
Exodus 12:1–28	Redemption: The Promise of Passover
Exodus 20:1–21	Redemption: The Ten Commandments
Leviticus 4:1–35	Redemption: The Sacrificial System
Isaiah 53	Redemption: Isaiah Foreshadows the Coming Promise
Luke 1:26–38; 2:1–20	Redemption: The Birth of Jesus
Matthew 3; John 1:29–34	Redemption: Jesus Is Baptized
Matthew 4:1–11	Redemption: The Temptation of Christ
John 3:1–21	Redemption: Jesus and Nicodemus
John 4:1–26, 39–42	Redemption: Jesus and the Woman at the Well
Luke 5:17–26	Redemption: Jesus Forgives and Heals
Mark 4:35–41	Redemption: Jesus Calms the Storm
Mark 5:1–20	Redemption: Jesus Casts Out Evil Spirits
John 11:1–44	Redemption: Jesus Raises Lazarus from the Dead
Matthew 26:26–30	Redemption: The First Lord's Supper
John 18:1–19:16	Redemption: Jesus Is Betrayed and Condemned
Luke 23:32–56	Redemption: Jesus Is Crucified
Luke 24:1–35	Redemption: Jesus Conquers Death
Luke 24:36–53	Redemption: Jesus Appears and Ascends
John 3:1–21	Redemption: We Have a Choice

NOTES

CHAPTER 3

1. See "Where Are the People DVD Preview," YouTube video, 7:21, a short preview of the American Church Research Project's Dave Olson's new DVD, posted by "theAmericanC," April 11, 2008 http://www.youtube.com/watch?v=vTvEuknfxVo.

CHAPTER 4

1. We got the phrase "Branded Christianity" from our friend Roy Moran.

2. "Number of Christians Rises, But Their Share of World Population Stays Stable," March 22, 2013, accessed August 5, 2014, http://www.pewresearch.org/daily-number/number-of-christians-rises-but-their-share-of-world-population-stays-stable/.

3. Rebecca Barnes and Lindy Lowry, "7 Startling Facts: An Up Close Look at Church Attendance in America," *ChurchLeaders* (blog), accessed August 5, 2014, http://www.churchleaders.com/pastors/pastor-articles/139575-7-startling-facts-an-up-close-look-at-church-attendance-in-america.html.

CHAPTER 12

1. *Serenity*, directed by Joss Whedon (Universal City, CA: Universal Pictures, 2005), motion picture.

MINISTRY AND MISSION RESOURCES

As you explore leading others on a journey of discovery and building spiritual leaders, check out these other great books that offer guidance from global experts on:

- Great Commission evangelism
- Obedience based discipleship
- Church planting
- Cross cultural ministry

MIRACULOUS MOVEMENTS	THE FATHER GLORIFIED	PRESSURE POINTS
9781418547288	9781418547301	9781418550745

THOMAS NELSON
Since 1798